# THE WONDER BOOK
## OF
# TELL ME WHY?

THE WIEILCZKA SALT MINES IN POLAND.

In this remarkable underground room, the chandelier and wall figures are made from salt.

**NATIVE HOUSE IN SUMATRA**

Elaborately carved and beautifully decorated, this picturesque dwelling is built on piles, in order to protect its inhabitants against the constant danger of floods. A large number of families live in it.

# THE WONDER BOOK

## OF

# TELL ME WHY?

*WITH SEVEN COLOUR PLATES AND*
*TWO HUNDRED AND FIFTY ILLUSTRATIONS*

*Seventh Edition*

WARD, LOCK & CO., LIMITED
LONDON AND MELBOURNE

# THE WONDER BOOK SERIES

## EACH WITH COLOUR PLATES AND
## HUNDREDS OF ILLUSTRATIONS

### THE WONDER BOOK OF BIBLE STORIES

Stories from the Old and New Testaments that live for ever, retold in an easily under-standable way for children. With 33 superb full-colour plates by Henry Coller and 100 line drawings by Dessau.

### THE WONDER BOOK OF THE FARM

Describes all modern farming and its place in our day-to-day life.

### THE WONDER BOOK OF AIRCRAFT

Describing and illustrating the wonderful strides that have been made in civil aviation.

### THE WONDER BOOK OF THE R.A.F.

All about our glorious Air Force and their marvellous machines.

### THE WONDER BOOK OF ANIMALS

This very popular volume is not merely a picture book, or a story book, or a natural history book, but a blend of all three, with many entertaining and instructive features.

### THE WONDER BOOK OF RAILWAYS

Scores of chatty articles about railways and locomotives all over the world.

### THE WONDER BOOK OF SHIPS

All about the great liners and other ships of the Merchant Navy.

### THE WONDER BOOK OF THE NAVY

All about the Navy of to-day.

### THE WONDER BOOK OF THE ARMY

Foreword by Field-Marshall VISCOUNT Montgomery of Alamein, K.G., G.C.B., D.S.O. Romance and adventure of the modern soldier at home and overseas.

### THE WONDER BOOK OF WHY & WHAT ?

Answers to children's questions on all sorts of subjects, with hundreds of pictures.

### THE WONDER BOOK OF WONDERS

The most wonderful things in the world fascinatingly described and illustrated.

### THE WONDER BOOK OF NATURE

Every child is at heart a lover of Nature and the open air. Boys and girls of all ages will be delighted with this volume.

### THE WONDER BOOK OF MOTORS

Aptly described as " the Rolls-Royce " of gift books.

### THE WONDER BOOK OF SCIENCE

Some of the most famous authorities tell the stories of modern discoveries and theories

### THE WONDER BOOK OF DO YOU KNOW ?

Tells in picture and story of some of the most wonderful things in the world—many of them in our own homes.

### THE WONDER BOOK OF TELL ME WHY ?

Answers to numbers of those puzzling questions that begin with the words How ? When ? Why ? and What ?

### THE WONDER BOOK OF HOW IT'S DONE

A brightly written and lavishly illustrated volume describing numbers of the interesting things a child sees in the course of a day, telling how they work, or how they are made.

### THE WONDER BOOK OF WOULD YOU BELIEVE IT ?

Many strange and wonderful things that are nevertheless true are described and illus-trated in this fascinating volume.

### THE WONDER BOOK OF THINGS TO DO

Provides not one solution, but many, to the perpetual question, " What can I do

### THE STORY WONDER BOOK

Delightful pictures and stories for boys and girls of all ages.

**MADE IN ENGLAND**
Printed in Great Britain by The Hollen Street Press Ltd., London, W.1.

AN ALBINO FITCH OR FERRET.                    [*Dorien Leigh, Ltd.*

# COLOUR PLATES

5

A CHINESE JUNK WITH FULL SAILS SET.

[B.O.A.C.

# PRINCIPAL CONTENTS

## ASTRONOMY AND NATURAL PHENOMENA

# CONTENTS

## BOTANY

## PHYSICS AND CHEMISTRY

[*Keystone.*

THE FEDSCHENKO GLACIER, AUSTRIA.
This being forty-eight miles long, is the largest glacier in the world, excluding those in the polar regions.

# CONTENTS

## PHYSICS AND CHEMISTRY (continued)

## GEOLOGY

THE SPEAKER'S CHAIR, HOUSE OF COMMONS, WESTMINSTER.
The Speaker is president and spokesman of the House, and has authority to keep order.

9

# CONTENTS

## HUMAN PHYSIOLOGY

## MACHINERY AND ENGINEERING

## ZOOLOGY

# CONTENTS

## ZOOLOGY (*continued*)

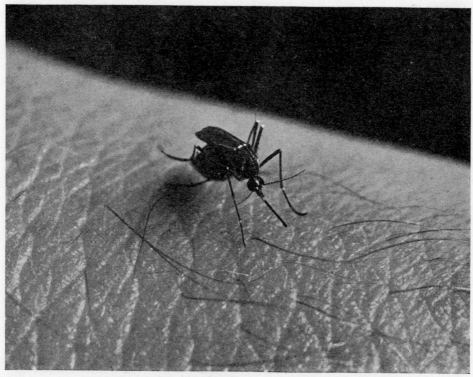

*[Shell Photographic Unit.*

A MOSQUITO PREPARING TO ENGORGE BLOOD.

# CONTENTS

## ZOOLOGY (*continued*)

## GENERAL

[*Tea Bureau.*

A PLAITED FROND OF COCONUT PALM; READY FOR THATCHING
A HOUSE IN CEYLON.

A BATHYSPHERE.

In this strange looking contrivance, it is possible to descend thousands of feet to the ocean bed.

# TELL ME WHY?

FROM the very beginning, men and women, boys and girls, have been asking, sometimes with their lips, more often only with their minds, " *Why ? Please tell me Why ?* "

Sometimes the questions can be answered, sometimes they cannot, for there are mysteries of Nature of which no one knows the secret, perhaps no one ever will.

But the *Why's* which *can* be answered, to some extent at least, are legion, and many of them are answered in this book and in its companion volumes, DO YOU KNOW? and WHY AND WHAT?, which lots of you already possess. What fun it is to take up almost any subject, even the most commonplace and "everyday," and find out little by little more and more about it ! Knowledge is like a snowball, the more you roll the faster the rate at which it grows.

13

A FILM ARTIST AT WORK.

Much of the preliminary work in the making of a Disney picture is done by " layout men."   The artist shown here is
laying out a background.   Layout men designate colour lighting, backgrounds and effects, prior to animation.

A SEA ANEMONE CATCHING A SMALL FISH. [F. Schensky.]

# HOW A SEA ANEMONE FEEDS?

WE can study the sea anemone in an aquarium, but we need not go far on the seashore before we see some of these lovely creatures, which have been called sea-flowers. They are found everywhere and are famous for their solitary life and their beautiful colours. They can move about from place to place ; one kind is carried on the shell of a hermit-crab. They are of many colours, red and green, and scarlet and tawny. Having no hard skeleton, they are able to change their shape quickly. They look, indeed, like lovely flowers, but their habits are not at all peaceful.

Sea anemones are carnivorous and can devour large pieces of flesh, and mussels and oysters. They stretch out their tentacles and gather in the food given them in the aquarium ; the tentacles carry crabs, fish or flesh into their mouth ; they can digest the flesh as well as the juices. They settle only where there is plenty of animal food. That is why they are found on rocky coasts, and why they use the crab as a kind of raft, for the crab goes where food is plentiful.

15

# WHAT IS THE SPHINX?

THE Sphinx, according to the English dictionary, is a representation of a fabulous winged monster of Egyptian origin, with a human or animal head, the body and paws of a lion and the tail of a serpent.

There are numerous forms of the Sphinx in existence, particularly in Egypt, but the one generally referred to as the Sphinx is the Great Sphinx at Giza. This, the most celebrated representation, is found in Egypt, not far from the Great Pyramid; it is a colossal female-headed monster carved out of solid limestone rock, one hundred and eighty-nine feet long and nearly sixty feet in height. Between its front paws is the entrance to a temple. It is so old that nothing is known as to the date of its construction. Some authorities think it is even older by far than its neighbour the Great Pyramid, which is believed to have been built six thousand years ago, while others declare that it must have been carved out about the same time that the Great Pyramid was erected, and that it was Chephren, son of Cheops, who built the Great Pyramid, who had the Great Sphinx carved out as the guardian of his tomb, which is in the Second Pyramid. This belief is substantiated by the fact that so many other sphinxes in Egypt appear to have been constructed as guardians to tombs.

The Greeks had a legend that the Sphinx was a female sea-monster who proposed riddles to the inhabitants of the city of Thebes, and those who could not supply the correct answers were strangled by her. ("Sphinx" is probably derived from a Greek word meaning "strangler.") The Thebans offered the throne of Thebes and the hand of their queen Jocasta to the man who would rid them for ever of the monster. One of her celebrated riddles was—

"What goes on four feet, two feet, and three,
But the more feet it goes on the weaker it be?"

Œdipus guessed the right answer—a man, who crawls on all-fours as a baby, walks upright when grown-up, and uses a stick in his old age.

The Sphinx was so disgusted at the success of Œdipus that in a fit of rage she strangled herself. And Œdipus married the queen and so became king of Thebes.

# WHY A SUMMER DAY IS LONGER THAN A WINTER DAY?

A SUMMER day is longer than a winter day because the sun is longer above the horizon in summer than winter. Besides spinning on its axis, the earth also circles round the sun once a year. The axis on which the earth spins is neither pointing at the sun nor upright with respect to the sun, but is inclined or tilted at an angle of sixty-six and a half degrees. The equator is the imaginary line which divides our world (the spherical earth) into two perfectly

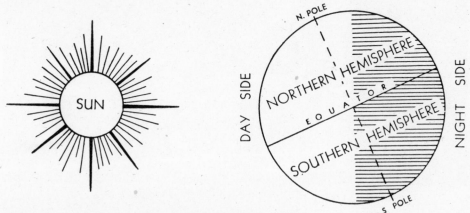

On June 21st of each year, the axis of the earth in the northern hemisphere is at its maximum tilt toward the sun. This is midsummer day in the northern hemisphere and midwinter in the southern hemisphere, with the south pole at its maximum inclination from the sun.

equal and opposite halves called hemispheres (half-spheres, hemi being Greek for half). During summer, the earth *spins with its axis tilted towards the sun* and this causes the sun to be longer above the horizon and to appear to describe a bigger circle in the heavens. When it is summer in one hemisphere, it is winter in the other. June 21st is midsummer day and the time of greatest tilt towards the sun for the inhabitants of the northern hemisphere. On this day the sun in Britain is over twice as long above the horizon as on December 21st, and at all places within the arctic circle there is daylight during the whole twenty-four hours. June 21st is midwinter day in the southern hemisphere, which is then most tilted away from the sun, and where there is as much night and darkness as there is day in the northern hemisphere. On December 21st the positions are exactly reversed.

See also: "Why is it dark at night?" page 136.

THE EMITRON TELEVISION CAMERA.

# WHAT WE REALLY SEE IN TELEVISION ?

IN Television we do not, of course, see the actual people and things at the transmitting end, any more than we hear the actual voices and musical instruments when we listen to our ordinary radio receiver.  In broadcasting the microphone changes the sound waves into electric signals which are in turn transmitted as radio waves through the ether to our receiver at home.  The received signals are amplified, and made to operate the loudspeaker which vibrates, and produces the sounds we would hear if we were in the studio.

In a similar way, the television camera changes light waves into electric signals, which are sent through the ether.  The television receiver changes the radio signals into light and shade, and builds up on a screen a reproduction of the scene we would see in the studio. The reproduction differs from the original not only in size but also in being black and white instead of coloured.  However, the time may

18

shortly come when even the colour of the scene will be reproduced.

One form of television camera, the Emitron, is illustrated on page 18. The scene to be televised is brought to a focus at a mica plate on which there are millions of photo-sensitive particles ; this plate can just be seen inside the bulb in the illustration. The action of light on this mosaic of particles is similar to its effect upon the cells at the back of the human eye. The light and shade of the televised scene reacts upon each photo-sensitive particle so that they become electrically charged : where the most light falls the charge is greatest. Nature has provided millions of nerves between the eye and the brain so that the light pattern on the eye cells can be transferred quickly. The television system has to transfer the electric charge pattern from the camera to the receiver just as quickly as the eye. However, it is impossible to provide the millions of wires which would be required from the transmitter so some other method must be found. The method devised for sending the charge pattern as separate signals over one path is known as " scanning ".

Each charged particle is considered in turn, the pattern of electric charges on the camera mosaic being scanned in a series of parallel paths, and a distinct signal is sent out as each spot is reached. The scanning is done by a beam of negatively charged particles. These negatively charged particles are called Electrons, and the long tube attached to the round bulb of the Emitron camera contains an arrangement known as an " electron gun ". This " gun " consists of an assembly of metal cylinders carrying very high voltages which cause a thin beam of electrons to be projected on the screen.

Special scanning circuits are arranged so that the beam sweeps backwards and forwards across the mica plate, just as you are reading this page: left to right slowly, then, right to left quickly to the next line. And in the same way that your eyes ignore the line which you have just read, when they sweep back to start the next one, so the electron beam is shut off when it moves back from right to left between each line.

To scan a complete picture the beam moves 405 times from left to right and it does this twenty-five times in one second. This means that the beam moves across the screen 10,125 times a second.

When the beam of negative electricity moves across the plate it neutralises the positive charges on the photo-sensitive particles and discharges them. Signals are passed through to a thin metal sheet on the back of the mica plate. These signals are amplified and made to vary very high frequency radio waves which are transmitted from the aerial. At the same time a microphone at the studio picks up the accompanying sound, which is changed to radio signals of another frequency. These signals operate the loudspeaker at the television receiver, thus the sound and vision signals are transmitted and received at the same time to give the complete programme.

On page 21 is an illustration showing the aerial tower of the Sutton Coldfield television transmitter. This tower is 750 feet high and transmits the television programmes relayed from London.

The vision radio signals are picked up on our home receiver and changed to points of light and dark which appear on the screen. The receiver screen is the bottom or flat end of a " cathode ray tube ", which is a large type of wireless valve, and consists of a glass envelope roughly in the shape of a flat bottomed bottle with a long neck ; the long neck contains an electron gun which projects a thin stream of electrons on the flat bottom which forms the picture screen. The bottom of the tube has a thin coating of a luminescent material which glows and gives off light when it is struck by an electron beam. The exact composition of the materials used on the screen by the manufacturers of cathode ray tubes is secret, but usually consists of a combination of zinc sulphide and zinc beryllium silicate.

The electron beam of the receiver is made to sweep across the luminescent screen in exact time with the electron beam in the television camera which is viewing the scene at the studio. Special circuits are provided to do this and special signals known as " synchronising signals " are sent from the transmitter to keep the sweep or scanning circuits of the receiver in time with those of the television camera.

The intensity or brightness of the light given off from the spot on the receiver screen depends upon the number of electrons reaching it. The number of electrons in the scanning beam is controlled by the signals received from the transmitter, so that the moving spot of light glows, or is darkened depending upon the signals received. When the electron beam of the camera is scanning a light part of the studio scene the received signal at our set allows the maximum number of electrons to reach the luminescent screen, and so a bright spot is registered. The received signal is changed when a dark spot is scanned by the camera so that the spot of light on the receiver screen is reduced in brightness.

In this way the picture on the receiver screen is built up of spots of light and shade, just as the newspaper illustration is made up of spots of different sizes, for if you examine any newspaper picture with a magnifying glass you will see that it consists of a pattern of dots, large and small.

If we were in the studio watching the performance, the light reflected from the actors and scenery would enter our eyes and fall upon the millions of tiny cells which form the back of the eye. These cells are connected by nerves to the brain, and when light falls upon them they send signals to it. The brain interprets these signals, and we experience the sensation of sight. The television camera works in a similar manner.

When we " look in " we think we see a complete picture, but it is only a small point of light, varying in brightness, and moving in a series of parallel lines across the screen. The spot or point of light moves so quickly that the impression it makes on the eye persists long enough to delude us.

By the time the spot has reached the end of the last scanning line at the bottom right-hand corner of the picture the first impression on the eye of the first line is just beginning to fade away.

A B.B.C. TRANSMITTING STATION
The aerial is at the top of a 750 feet mast.

# WHY OWLS FLY SILENTLY?

THE owl is described as "a large-headed, small-faced, hook-beaked, large-eyed, soft-plumaged, nocturnal bird of prey." We might add to this that it is a bird whose cry we hear at night-time from some church-tower or barn or trees. But the most important thing to remember is the food upon which this bird lives.

[Fox Photos.

A GREAT EAGLE OWL WITH HER TWO EGGS.

To get that food it needs its hooked beak and its large eyes in front, which can look down in the dark and see things we should miss. The owl feeds entirely on living creatures such as rats and mice and birds and snails ; and to find them it goes out at night.

But imagine this big bird with wings which made a loud flapping noise. All the rats and mice, and even the snails, would get a warning that it was coming, and would hide or escape. The owl is able, however, to move silently because its feathers are soft and light, and so constructed that the air cannot " whistle " through them as in other birds.

22

# WHY ARE FLOWERS OF DIFFERENT COLOURS?

The Sloe is one of the first plants to invite insects to its flowers.

WITHOUT insects the world would, indeed, be a sombre place, for there would scarcely be a coloured flower to gladden our eyes.

That floral colours should please us is interesting, but it is for insects' eyes that those colours are really produced.

Plants need aid of insects to pollinate their blooms, and like competitive tradesmen, they have to advertise. Each display of coloured petals is simply a bold announcement to flying insects that prime, sweet nectar, or rich pollen, may there be obtained.

Since there are many kinds of insects with entirely different tastes, it follows that special colours have a particular appeal. Consequently, those plants which require bees to pollinate their flowers, specialise in purple and blue-violet.

Yellow and red flowers have little or no attraction for the bees. Recent experiments have shown that bees are blind to red ; to them it means black—just as it does to a photographic plate.

More amazing still ; it is found that they can see the ultra - violet, which, though invisible to our eyes, affects a photographic plate.

Bees do sometimes visit what we term red flowers, but such flowers always have some mixture of various other colours.

*Photos]*                                             *[John J. Ward.*

The Dog Rose attracts all kinds of insects with its pale pink flowers. It does not provide nectar, but supplies abundant pollen.

# WHY SUNSHINE IS HOTTEST AT THE EQUATOR?

SUNSHINE is hottest at the equator because it falls more nearly vertical there all the year round than anywhere else. When anything strikes us, we get the full hundred per cent force behind it only if it comes straight at us and scores a direct hit. This is true whether it be heat rays shot out by the sun at the earth or stones thrown by a small boy at a pane of glass. Sunshine from a vertical sun (*i.e.*, a sun immediately or vertically over our heads) scores an absolute direct hit at the earth's surface, and only upon and near to the equator (*i.e.*, within the tropics), is a vertical sun ever to be seen. At all other places in the world, the sun is always lower down in the sky, his beams thus always fall more or less obliquely, and oblique or slanting rays are always less powerful because they are more diffused; they are less effective than vertical rays just as glancing blows are less effective than direct hits. In January the earth receives seven per cent more light and heat from the sun than it does in July—because in January the earth is three million miles

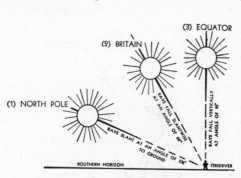

nearer the sun than in July. Yet Britain is 23°F. colder in January than in July. Why? In Britain in July the sun at noon is about four times higher up in the heavens and its rays consequently reach us in a direction four times more upright. Low suns give us winter; high suns give us summer.

# HOW FAST A BULLET MOVES?

A BULLET from a modern military rifle leaves the muzzle at the extraordinary high speed of 2,440 feet per second, or more than 1,650 miles an hour. But wind resistance at such a high speed is very great, and although a bullet starts with a speed of 2,440 feet per second, it only travels 1,800 feet in the first second. In the next second the distance travelled is reduced to 1,200 feet, while in the third second it is only about 900 feet. At a range of two miles, the bullet can do little more than drop on its target.

THIS WIRELESS OPERATOR MAINTAINS GROUND TO AIR CONTACT
AT AN EQUATORIAL AIRPORT IN AFRICA.

25

STORING BLOCK SALT IN A WAREHOUSE.

# WHERE SALT COMES FROM ?

ALL the rocks and soil of the earth contain a little salt, and as these are washed and worn away by rain and rivers, the salt is dissolved and carried to the sea or some inland lake. The oceans are always evaporating to form clouds and rain, but they cannot part with anything but pure water, so any salt they contain must stay behind, and this is always being added to. If, by any chance, the sea is evaporating so fast that it is gradually drying up, like the inland seas of the Caspian, Ural, and Dead Sea, then the water becomes more and more salty, until there comes a time when it cannot hold all its salt in solution. Then crystals appear and form a solid layer beneath the brine. This may be covered with mud and preserved, and then other layers of salt may be formed in the same way, one above the other, with layers of mud between. This is how the layers of salt which are found in Cheshire in England, Stassfurt in Germany and other places, have been formed, for ages ago there were inland seas or salt-lakes which dried up and left deposits of salt behind. Salt is often taken out of the mines in solid blocks, but more often water is poured down the mine to dissolve the salt, and the brine is then pumped to the surface, where it is evaporated in tanks and the salt recovered.

26

["*Topical*" *Press.*

SCRAPING THE ROUGH PORTIONS FROM BLOCKS OF SALT.

A DISNEY "ANIMATOR" WORKING ON A SKETCH OF PECOS BILL.

# HOW ARE MICKEY MOUSE AND SILLY SYMPHONY FILMS MADE?

WE know that when we are looking at an ordinary cinematograph film we are seeing a series of photographs of an actual incident or scene. We know, too, that sometimes there may be a great deal of make-believe about what we see ; the massive castle wall, for instance, is perhaps made of lath and plaster, and it may be that the hero has not really risked his life in quite such a daring manner as he seems to have done, although cinematograph actors often do perform most wonderful and daring feats. All the same, we realise that there *was* a castle wall of sorts, and there *was* a living person playing the part of the hero. But as we sit and chuckle at the amusing adventures and hair-breadth escapes of Mickey Mouse and his wife Minnie, or any of the other delightful and mysterious characters in the Silly Symphonies—well, the thought may come to us suddenly, " Oh, yes, but such persons *do not exist* !

# HOW ARE MICKEY MOUSE FILMS MADE?

How can it be possible to make photographs of them for the film?"
The explanation of this apparent impossibility is very simple. You
are looking at a series of drawings which have been photographed
one after each other, each successive drawing showing a slight
forward motion in the action of the figures represented. Now,
when you learn that a film four hundred feet in length requires
over six thousand photographs, you can see that it would take an
artist many months to make that enormous number of pictures. So
the following ingenious method is devised to reduce that number.
Let us imagine that a policeman standing still but waving an arm
is represented. A picture of him will be made *omitting this arm* ;
next, on sheets of transparent material a series of sketches of his
arm will be drawn, each showing a slight movement. Then, in
turn, photographs of the policeman are taken one after the other
with his " different arms " in proper order placed on the top of the
original drawing. Even when this " short cut " is used a very
large number of drawings is required, and if the policeman moves
more than his one arm, or he moves away from his background,
or if other characters are introduced, then it is necessary to have a new
original main drawing and the photograph must start all over again.

THE FAMOUS WALT DISNEY MULTIPLANE CRANE.
The camera shoots down on transparent material, giving a feeling of dimension to a scene. A full crew are here
checking the scenes and backgrounds.

# WHAT CAUSES YOU TO "SEE STARS"?

WHEN you use one of your five senses, you are able to do so because the special nerve attached to that sense becomes "excited" or "stimulated" and carries the impression to the brain, which interprets and tells *you* the result. Someone puts a finger on your skin; the brain tells you someone has "touched" you. Another puts a rose under your nose, and the brain tells you you are "smelling" a scented rose—and so on. Each special nerve can carry only the impression of its special sense. A "touch" nerve cannot convey "sound," or the "hearing" nerve "sight"; but if you damage one of them, say by pricking, you get "sight," "sound," or some other sensation, according to which is pricked. So you if get a smack on your eye, the sudden pressure on your eyeball "stimulates" the "sight" nerve, and the brain, getting the impression through that nerve, tells *you* that you see light; and so you do, in the form of light specks which do not really exist—you "see stars"!

The "pain" you might feel at the same time is caused by the "stimulation" of the "touch" nerves in the skin about your eye.

# HOW PLANTS BREATHE?

DURING daylight every green plant is absorbing carbonic acid gas and exhaling oxygen, which is just the reverse of animal respiration. At night the plant ceases to absorb carbonic acid gas, and also to exhale oxygen. It is then found to be breathing in the animal way.

The truth is that the plant's absorption of carbonic acid gas and exhaling of oxygen is its feeding process. It requires the carbon from that gas, and returns to the air the oxygen it contains. Throughout the day it is also breathing in the ordinary animal manner, but the oxygen exhaled in its feeding process conceals that it is also exhaling carbonic acid gas.

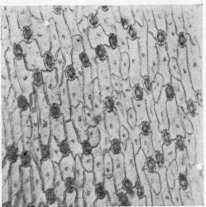

[*John J. Ward.*

Stomata, or breathing pores, on the leaf of a tulip. These remain open by day, when the plant is feeding from the air, and closed at night.

30

STAR CLOUDS IN SAGITTARIUS.

STONEHENGE IN WILTSHIRE, PROBABLY THE MOST FAMOUS MONUMENT
OF ANTIQUITY IN THE BRITISH ISLES.

[B.O.A.C.

IN SICILY THE HUMBLEST CART IS BEAUTIFULLY DECORATED.

THE 200-INCH TELESCOPE AT THE OBSERVATORY ON MOUNT PALOMAR

THE PUYA PLANT OF SOUTH AMERICA

Found in the Bolivian Andes, the puya plant, a relative of the pineapple, blooms once in 150 years, and then dies.
The flower head is sometimes 24 feet long, 8 feet in circumference, and may contain 8,000 flowers.

SETTING AN "INVISIBLE RAY" ALARM.

[*Mirrorpic.*

# WHAT IS AN INVISIBLE RAY?

WHEN we speak of " light," we usually mean white light, which, although it is itself invisible, makes visible things upon which it falls. The " beam " of light we see coming through a window into a darkened room is not actually light, but millions of illuminated dust particles. There are other kinds of light which do not make the articles from which they are reflected visible to the human eye. These kinds of light have wavelengths either longer or shorter than those forming the comparatively small group we call the " visible spectrum ".

One of these types of light is the infra-red. It is longer than the red of the visible spectrum and does not " illuminate " anything it touches. A hot iron in a dark room might be faintly visible because of the red rays emitted, but actually, it is giving off a great deal of invisible infra-red rays. Ultra-violet rays are also beyond the range of the visible spectrum and therefore do not normally render objects visible to the eye. There are many other kinds of " light " which we cannot detect, but of whose existence we can be sure.

If we cannot see these invisible rays, how do we know they exist ?  For one thing, they act on our skins, and for another, we can take photographs by them.  Because they are considerably more penetrating, infra-red and ultra-violet rays enable us to take photographs " in the dark " through objects which might be " solid " to ordinary light.  Recently, the " invisible ray " has been used for working a photo-electric cell.  A visible light beam would do as well, but for burglar alarms, the invisible ray is obviously more effective.  For other purposes, too, it is more convenient, or we should have doors opening and bells ringing as soon as we switched on the electric light !

[Kodak, Ltd.

An infra-red record, taken in total darkness, of an operator examining film by means of an infra-red viewing device. The operator can see the film, which would be spoiled by white light, and the camera can see the whole picture, but to the unaided eye all is in pitch darkness.

## AN INVISIBLE RAY MACHINE.

[*Mirrorpic*.

This model of a wagon and two horses was placed on a brilliantly lit miniature stage. The ray machine was set in operation and suddenly at the head of the two horses a third horse appeared from nowhere.

# WHAT COLOUR MAKES LIFE POSSIBLE?

OUT of all the colours of the rainbow there is one that means life to every man, horse, dog, sheep, bullock, and, indeed, every other animal on the earth. The fresh green of springtime may suggest which colour it is. But the power of green lies very much deeper than that. Plants, alone in all the universe, have the power of building up starch from carbon dioxide, which is the waste gas we breathe out, and water. They, at the same time, produce oxygen. No chemist has yet been able to imitate their achievement. But we do know that a green colouring matter, called chlorophyll, and sunlight play essential parts in the process. Without chlorophyll there would be no growth in the vegetable world. Without vegetable growth, we should be deprived not only of flour and bread and potatoes, but mutton and beef as well. Even flesh-eating animals are ultimately dependent on the chlorophyll of plants for their food. Next to life itself, chlorophyll is the most wonderful thing in the world. It makes life possible.

# WHAT IS "HEAVY" WATER?

"HEAVY" water is a poison, but you drink it every day. There is, in fact, nothing rare or miraculous about "heavy" water, although, it has been discovered only so lately. It is to be found mixed, in minute proportion, with any ordinary water. Indeed, there must be millions of millions of tons in the sea alone. The only difficulty is to separate it from the ordinary water with which it is mixed. Ordinary water is made of hydrogen, which is an explosive gas, and oxygen. "Heavy" water differs from ordinary water just in this, that the atoms of hydrogen which it contains are twice as heavy as those of ordinary hydrogen. "Heavy" water is, therefore, itself heavier than ordinary water, but in a smaller proportion, actually about one part in ten. One result of this extra weight is that any large proportion of "heavy" water appears likely to upset the delicate chemical balance which controls the working of our bodies, and, indeed, any form of life. "Heavy" water will, for example, kill tadpoles and prevent seeds from germinating. If we drink nothing but "heavy" water, we should certainly die.

# IS A WHALE A FISH?

THE whale looks like a big fish ; it moves in the water like a fish ; it has a big head and no distinct neck, just like a fish. But it is a mammal, a warm-blooded animal ; it has a heart in four parts and it breathes with lungs. The mother whale produces her young alive and feeds them herself ; indeed, she is a most affectionate mother. The majority of whales are harmless and even timid creatures. It seems certain that they have become so much like fishes because they wanted

[*Mirrorpic.*

TWO WHALES BREAKING SURFACE NEAR A " CHASER."

to move through the water ; the shape of the fish is the best suited to this movement. But whales are not now, and never were, fishes.

There are many species of whale, but apart from differences in size, the general appearance is the same. Whales are divided into two types—whalebone whales and toothed whales. The largest species of whale, which is known as the Rorqual or Right Finback, and which comes in the first category, may be as much as a hundred feet long and much heavier than the biggest elephant, which is the largest of the land mammals.

A whale does not chew its food, but swallows it whole—even if it is eating a cuttlefish or seal !

[E.N.A.

THE EFFECT OF AN EARTHQUAKE ON A BLOCK OF FLATS.

A JAPANESE STREET AFTER AN EARTHQUAKE.

# WHAT CAUSES AN EARTHQUAKE?

AN earthquake is a series of waves which spreads out in all directions from a central source of disturbance. These waves, or oscillations, are *land* waves, or *rock* waves, just as waves at sea are water waves, and they can be caused by any blow or sudden movement of objects or materials. The slipping of surface rocks under gravity ; the flow of molten rock under the cool, hard, outer crust of the earth ; the multiple high-speed motions of the earth itself ; sudden alterations of temperature and barometric pressure ; storms and the tides. These things, and a score of others, combine to impose a terrific all-round strain and keep the earth's surface incessantly quivering like a giant fly-wheel.

It is not surprising, therefore, that *over fifty thousand earthquakes are recorded every year*, the overwhelming majority of which, happily, are small and harmless.

A GIANT BUDDHA IN TOKIO.

The modern air traveller may see a sight such as this within a matter of hours.

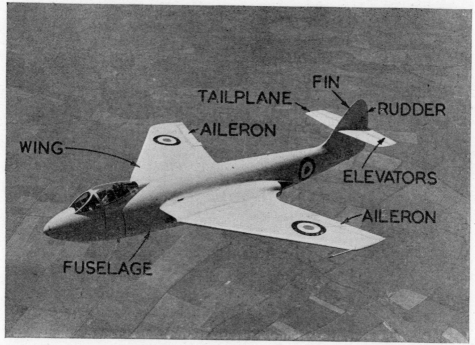

FIG. 1. CHIEF COMPONENTS OF AN AEROPLANE.

# HOW AN AEROPLANE FLIES?

THE chief components of an aeroplane are shown in FIG. 1, where it will be seen that the conventional machine has two horizontal surfaces called wings which act to support the weight of the aircraft and keep it stable and a smaller vertical surface (the fin and rudder) which is mainly responsible for controlling the *direction* of flight, all these being joined to the fuselage in a definite order. The propeller is rotated rapidly by the power of the engine and draws the whole machine forward and it is this forward motion of the aeroplane which produces the necessary lift to support the weight of the whole machine. Each of the wing surfaces, it will be noticed, has a smaller movable surface incorporated which is responsible for control and manœuvrability.

The forces acting on an aeroplane in flight are shown in FIG. 2. The propeller thrust pulls the machine forwards. This motion means that air is flowing past the wings and, by virtue of the actual shape of these wings and the angle at which they meet this stream of air, a powerful upward force is generated which is sufficient to support the weight of the whole aircraft.

What actually happens to produce this *lift* force is shown in FIG. 3. Air meeting the front or leading edge of the wing is parted, one section flowing over the top surface and one over the under surface. A wing section is so shaped that the distance from the front edge to the rear edge (trailing edge) is greater over the top surface than over the bottom surface so that in order to meet again at the trailing edge the stream of air flowing over the *top* surface must travel *faster*.

The fact that the air flowing over the top surface is travelling faster means that it is exerting less pressure on the top surface than on the bottom surface and so an upward force is generated, which is called the *lift* force. This effect is increased by inclining the wing upwards so that the leading edge is higher than the trailing edge, but only up to a point. When this angle of inclination reaches a certain figure (about 15 degrees roughly for a conventional section) the air no longer flows smoothly over the top surface but breaks

[*Chas. G. Brown.*

FIG. 2. THE FORCES ACTING ON AN AEROPLANE IN FLIGHT.

away and lift *decreases*. The wing is then said to be in a stalled condition.

Part of the lift force is generated by air striking the inclined air flowing over the top surface, which is why lift falls off so rapidly once a stalled condition is reached.

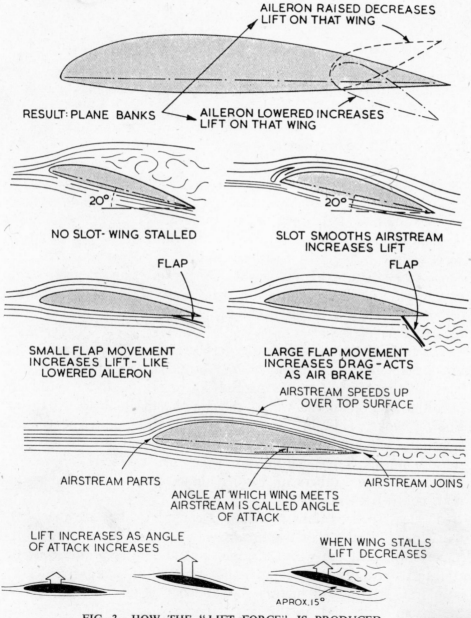

AILERON RAISED DECREASES LIFT ON THAT WING

RESULT: PLANE BANKS

AILERON LOWERED INCREASES LIFT ON THAT WING

20°

NO SLOT- WING STALLED

20°

SLOT SMOOTHS AIRSTREAM INCREASES LIFT

FLAP

SMALL FLAP MOVEMENT INCREASES LIFT- LIKE LOWERED AILERON

FLAP

LARGE FLAP MOVEMENT INCREASES DRAG - ACTS AS AIR BRAKE

AIRSTREAM SPEEDS UP OVER TOP SURFACE

AIRSTREAM PARTS

ANGLE AT WHICH WING MEETS AIRSTREAM IS CALLED ANGLE OF ATTACK

AIRSTREAM JOINS

LIFT INCREASES AS ANGLE OF ATTACK INCREASES

WHEN WING STALLS LIFT DECREASES

APROX. 15°

FIG. 3. HOW THE "LIFT FORCE" IS PRODUCED

Now a wing on its own is not stable. When drawn through the air it would have a natural tendency to increase its angle of attack until it stalled, so another horizontal aerofoil called the tailplane is used to control this tendency and keep the wing at an efficient flying attitude. The tailplane is fitted with movable surfaces called elevators, which are controlled by the pilot, so that he can adjust the machine to fly at just what attitude he requires.

To fly fast, the pilot trims the aeroplane to fly with the wings at a very small angle of attack, so that the *drag* of the wings is as small as possible. How fast the machine can go is a matter of how much thrust is available from the propeller (or jet engine) to balance the drag of the whole aeroplane. As speed increases, drag also increases until a point is reached where the two are equal and the aeroplane can go no faster.

To fly slowly the pilot raises the elevators to raise the nose of the machine and thus increase the angle of attack of the wings for more lift and decreases the thrust by throttling back the engine to balance the new drag value at this speed and flight attitude. If he now increases the thrust (opens the throttle), or simply raises the elevators when flying at a higher speed, more lift is produced than is necessary to support the weight of the aircraft and it gains height or climbs. Similarly, depressing the elevators lowers the nose and decreases the angle of attack of the wings (and thus the list) and the machine dives.

To turn, the pilot uses both ailerons and rudder. The ailerons operate differently. That is, as one is raised, the other is lowered. This has the effect of increasing and decreasing the lift, respectively, over the portion of the wings, causing the machine to tip to one side or *bank*. This, in conjunction with rudder movement which steers the whole aeroplane in the direction on bank, results in a smooth turn. Some aeroplanes will turn correctly on aileron movement alone, others on rudder alone, but it is general to use both controls together.

Devices such as flaps and slots are used to increase the lift of the wings. Slots delay the break-away of the airstream from the upper surface of the wings at high angles of attack and allow the wings to go on lifting up to an angle of attack of twenty-five degrees or more. Flaps both increase lift and act as an airbrake to slow the machine up and are therefore particularly useful for landing.

# HOW AN AEROPLANE FLIES ?

Small flap angles give increased lift with little increase in drag. Larger flap angles give little increase in lift, but a considerable amount of drag to slow the machine up.

[*Mirrorpic.*

**A NICE SLICE OF ROAST TURKEY.**

OSTRICHES RUNNING. [*South African Railways*

# HOW FAST CAN ANIMALS RUN?

IT is not easy to time other animals so well as we can time man. The stop-watch tells that a very good runner has done the 100-yards race in ten seconds. For that distance he is running at nearly twenty-one miles an hour. But if he has a mile to run, he can do only fourteen miles an hour. How does that compare with a race-horse or a greyhound? A race-horse will go much faster than a man, but is slower than an ostrich. The race-horse goes from thirty-two to thirty-eight miles an hour, and the ostrich sixty. But when we think of such creatures as the ostrich, we can't use the stop-watch. Man is not by any means a swift animal, but being able to use his mind and his hands, he has made machines which carry him faster than the ostrich. Clearly, an animal, like man, who carries so much weight on two legs, starts at a disadvantage. Man does not need to move so quickly. Other creatures have to possess a great deal of swiftness, partly because they may need to escape from the attack of their enemies, and also because they must find their food by quick movements.

46

# WHAT IS THE GIANT'S CAUSEWAY?

AGES ago there were great volcanic eruptions in the West of Scotland and North of Ireland, and great sheets of liquid lava covered the surface of the country. When lava cools and becomes solid, it contracts, and this tendency to get smaller naturally starts at the top of the sheet, which is in contact with the cool air, and at the bottom, which rests upon the cool earth. When such a sheet tries to get smaller, and cannot move as a whole, it cracks, and these cracks will break the sheet up into regular shapes that will have as many sides as possible. You will see, if you try it, that six-sided shapes (hexagons) are those with the greatest number of sides which will fit together without leaving irregular spaces. As the cooling of the lava went on and the sheet got solid towards the middle, these hexagonal cracks travelled inwards and in the end the sheet of lava appeared like a great mass of six-sided pillars fitted

[*Travel Association Photograph.*

THE GIANT'S CAUSEWAY.

47

closely together. If you look at a puddle of mud which is drying up after rain, you will often see that, as it dries and shrinks, it cracks up into little six-sided pillars. The Giant's Causeway in Antrim and the Island of Staffa with Fingal's Cave in Scotland are both fine examples of a lava flow from a volcano which has had six-sided columns produced in it by its shrinking as it cooled and became solid. The Giant's Causeway is so called because the ends of the columns as seen on the flat shore look like an enormous but carefully designed pavement.

# WHAT FISH USES A ROD AND LINE?

DEEP down in the depths of the ocean are to be found a host of weird creatures whose existence, long suspected and imagined, has only in recent years been definitely established. Among these strange creatures are several species of Angler Fish, extraordinary and grotesque creatures, actually furnished with their own rod and line for the purpose of catching other smaller fish.

The species illustrated below is known as *Gigantactis macronema*. Its " line " is actually four times the length of its body and at its tip it carries an illuminated lure. The picture is of one of the remarkable models of deep-sea fish made for the Fish gallery of the British Museum of Natural History, South Kensington. Another species, known as *Lasiognathus saccostoma*, appears on page 49.

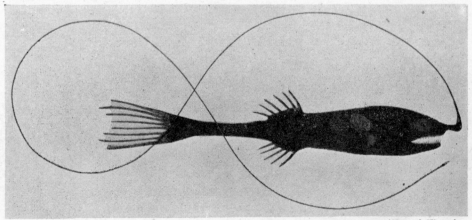

By permission of]                                    [*The British Museum (Natural History).*

A DEEP-SEA ANGLER FISH, *GIGANTACTIS MACRONEMA.*

**ANOTHER DEEP-SEA ANGLER FISH, *LASIOGNATHUS SACCOSTOMA*, WITH ROD, LINE, BAIT AND HOOKS.**

# TELL ME, PLEASE ?

1.  What is the meaning of the name Peter?

2.  What is meant by " A cock-and-bull story "?

3.  What is the difference between an apiary and an aviary?

4.  What are the " Steppes "?

5.  Who slept with a stone as a pillow?

6.  Whom did ravens feed?

7.  In what game is the word " bias " used?

8.  What do we mean by a stymie?

9.  What is a chukker?

10.  What is a " Marathon " race?

11.  What do we mean by the " Ashes "?

12.  Who are the " All Blacks " ?

*For answers to these questions see page 50.*

# ANSWERS TO QUESTIONS on page 49

1. A stone.

2. An obviously untrue story.

3. In an apiary are kept bees ; in an aviary, birds.

4. Elevated, barren regions in Northern Russia and Siberia.

5. Jacob.

6. Elijah.

7. Bowls.

8. When the ball of one golfer obstructs that of another player on a hole.

9. A period of play during a polo match.

10. A running race over a long distance ; so named after Pheidippides' run to Athens after the battle of Marathon.

11. The trophy played for at the Cricket Test Matches between England and Australia.

12. A Rugby football team representing New Zealand.

[*Tea Bureau.*

AN ESKIMO CARRYING PRECIOUS FUEL.

[Tea Bureau.

The Eskimo in the centre is melting snow to make tea.   The igloo can be seen in the background.

# WHAT IS AN IGLOO?

AN Igloo is a hut constructed by the Eskimo Indians for their winter quarters.  There is no wood obtainable in vast stretches of their country (which lies to the extreme north of America ; they also inhabit the shores of Greenland), and they make use of snow—the only building material available.  The Eskimo digs a trench in a freshly-fallen snowdrift and then proceeds to cut out blocks with his bone knife.  These blocks are slightly curved, and he arranges them so as to form a beehive-shaped hut, filling up the crevices and cracks with loose snow.  So expert are the Eskimos that a small house can be built in a couple of hours.  Then the door opening is plugged with skins and a blubber-oil lamp is lit so that the inside surface of the hut melts slightly.  At the right moment the skins are removed from the doorway and the cold air outside rushes in and a coating of ice forms on the walls.  In a little while the entire structure becomes solid ice, and the igloo is so strong that the dome-shaped roof will bear the weight of a hungry polar bear if it comes sniffing round in search of food.  Lastly, when " beds " have been installed—these are platforms of snow—the house is ready for occupation, and though we should find the absence of ventilation very trying, the Eskimos are quite contented with their snug but stuffy winter homes.

# WHAT IS A NEBULA?

NEBULA is the Latin word for a cloud or mist and in astronomy refers to a huge cloud of stars or glowing gas. Very few indeed can be seen with the naked eye and they look like fuzzy little patches of faint white light. The great or spiral nebulae have been called also " island universes " on account of their vastness. About two million are visible in the tremendous Mount Wilson telescope, and each one is at least one thousand million times heavier than the sun, which in turn is itself three hundred thousand times heavier than the whole earth. Nebulae are, however, composed of gases so un-

The great nebula of Andromeda as photographed with the two-foot reflector of the Yerkes Observatory. An exposure of four hours was given.

believably light and rarefied that a chunk of them about the size of a battle-ship weighs less than a speck of dust on a spider's web. Many have whirled themselves into a striking spiral shape by very rapid rotation. Photographed flat or full-on, these remind one of mam-

moth catherine-wheel fireworks. Hence the term spiral. Our photographs on this and next page show the great nebula of Andromeda and a remarkable nebula south of Zeta Orionis. Their distances are more awe-inspiring than their size. *Nearest* is over 5,000,000,000,000,000,000 (five trillion or million million million) miles away. Very faint spiral nebulae in the constellation of Gemini are the most remote objects discovered in the universe. A wireless signal reaches Australia from England in $\frac{1}{15}$ of a sec. Flashed from the earth today, a wireless signal would not reach these nebulae *till after a lapse of 150 million years.*

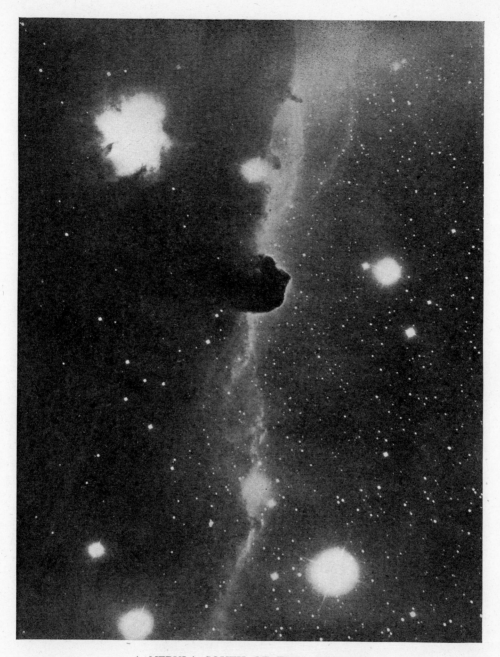

## A NEBULA SOUTH OF ZETA ORIONIS.

This photograph was taken with a three hours' exposure through a 100-inch reflector. In the centre will be seen a great projection, or dark bay, cutting off the light from behind. Nebulae are almost innumerable. About ten million are visible in the 100-inch Mount Wilson telescope. The majority are so huge as to be incomprehensible to the human mind. They are formed of incandescent gaseous matter and appear as dim, luminous, cloud-like areas in the sky.

# HOW WASPS MAKE PAPER?

THAT wasps make paper you can see for yourselves. If you study a wasp's nest, you will see that it is shaped like a football, and within it there are very many cells. These are protected by the paper made by the wasps out of wood. The nest begins with the queen ; she is the first to make ready for the colony. Early in the spring she sends out her first company of workers, who help to find food and make the growing nest, which is placed in a hole in the ground or in a hollow tree. The worker-wasp comes to the

H. Bastin]        Mondiale.
### A WASP'S NEST.

trunk of a dead tree or to a post or a fence ; it scrapes off a little of the wood with its sharp jaws ; it moistens this with its tongue, and kneads it as a woman does when she makes bread. So it becomes really paper, and while it is soft it can be made any shape that is required. You can see this paper stretched across the nest and also made into pillars, which hang downward and bind the rows together. Wasps are known to use cartridge paper which they find ready made. If you wait quietly, some day in early summer, you will see these paper-makers at work.

# WHY IRON GOES RUSTY?

CORROSION is nature's slow fire, and a very destructive sort of fire it is. But, whereas combustible materials in an ordinary fire are merely oxidised, that is, combined with oxygen, metals when they corrode form hydroxides, that is, they combine with water as well as oxygen. The basis of all corrosion is unquestionably electrical, but we must look to other causes if we want to know why one metal or alloy corrodes badly and another does not. Some metals are certainly protected by a thin impervious skin of hydroxide. Rust flakes off readily and so corrosion can eat ever deeper into the iron.

# WHAT IS THE DIFFERENCE BETWEEN A BUTTERFLY AND A MOTH?

A<sup>T</sup> once we say quite rightly that butterflies are out in the day, flying in the sunshine, while it is at night that we see the moths drawn to the lamp-post or other lights. But there are other differences. Both have antennæ, that is, feelers, but the butterfly's are fine but clubbed at the end, the moth's are broad and furry and pointed at the end. Both are caterpillars before they fly as we know them.

When a butterfly settles, it generally rests with the wings closed, that is, folded together so that top side touches top side (as in the picture), while a moth at rest either has the wings wrapped around its body, or folded to form a kind of roof on its abdomen, or spread out horizontally.

Both butterflies and moths are members of the same order of four-winged insects—known as *Lepidoptera*. Unlike moths, butterflies often resemble their surroundings—leaves, bark, flowers, etc. This " mimicry " is intended to render them invisible to their enemies.

*[Harold Bastin.*

### A BUTTERFLY AT REST.
Note the " protective resemblance " to its surroundings.

[*Shell Photographic Unit.*

A FLY'S HEAD.

# DO PLANTS FEEL ?

SINCE plants do not possess a brain, or main nerve centre, they cannot feel in the sense that animals do.

Nevertheless, some plants are provided with specialized cells which promptly respond to external vibrations.

There is the Sensitive Plant (*Mimosa pudica*) of Brazil, which, should you, when near to it, suddenly spread your umbrella, will instantly close its leaflets together and let its leaf stalks fall, as if alarmed by the movement.

Indeed, in bright sunlight, even your shadow falling on its leaves will cause them to droop slightly, while a gentle touch or a puff of air from your lips will make the whole plant shrink like a frightened animal.

Such sensitive plants " go to sleep," or droop their leaves, at the decline of light—as in the wood-sorrel and clovers. From this beginning of " closing shop " at night-fall, the sensitive habit was probably evolved.

[*Harold Bastin.*

SENSITIVE PLANT BEFORE TOUCHING.  SENSITIVE PLANT AFTER TOUCHING.

57

# HOW DO WE GET OIL FROM THE EARTH?

OIL can be got from the earth by mining and by boring—two different methods. Petroleum is sometimes found in shale, which is a rock substance which splits into sheets like slate and when ground and heated in a still, gives off a mineral oil—shale oil. The bulk of the oil we use is petroleum, which is obtained from deep wells in America and Asia. An iron pipe is driven through the soil (generally sandy) and a drill inside is rotated and water, led under pressure by a pipe to the drill, brings up the displaced material till oil is reached, sometimes at a depth of four thousand feet. When the drill strikes an underground stratum containing oil confined under pressure, the oil rushes up, flinging drills, tools, etc., out, and spurts up in a dense column of oil shooting two or three hundred feet into the air. Such wells are called "gushers." Other wells

[Anglo-Iranian Oil Co., Ltd.

A DRILLING CREW AT WORK IN SOUTH IRAN.

REFUELLING AN AIRLINER.    [*B.O.A.C.*

have to be pumped, and gushers which in time fail to gush can still supply oil if pumped by steam pumps.

If a well begins to show signs of failing, a " torpedo " comprising a heavy charge of explosive is fired (by an electric spark at the end of a cable) at the bottom of the well and results in a quickened flow of oil.

The oil is conveyed from the wells by pipe-lines, sometimes as much as six hundred miles long, to coast or railway.

Petroleum itself is an evil-smelling, greenish black liquid. It is generally believed to consist of the decayed parts of tiny sea creatures. By a process of distillation, the crude petroleum is separated into a number of useful oils, including petrol, paraffin oil, light and heavy naptha, paraffin wax, lubricating oil and petroleum jelly.

We need petrol to drive our cars, paraffin oil to light lamps and stoves, paraffin wax to make candles, and petroleum jelly to soothe sore lips and burns, so it can be seen that petroleum is very important to us indeed.

The article on Artesian Wells (see page 93) describes the manner in which the wells are bored.

# HOW AN ELECTRIC LAMP GIVES LIGHT?

WHEN a piece of metal is heated, the energy begins to be radiated as heat and light, the light radiated first becomes visible at the temperature we call " red heat ", but there is much more light at " white heat." In an electric lamp a fine metal wire, or filament, is heated, either in a vacuum or an " atmosphere " of an inert gas. The vacuum would seem to be better because less energy is lost by radiation of the heat ; theoretically there should be no loss at all. An inert gas, that is to say, a gas such as argon which will not react chemically with the metal even at high temperatures, is better still because it makes it possible to heat up the metal further and to obtain a brighter light even if extra heat is wasted.

The metal most often used for filaments, either alone or with others, is tungsten, because of its very high melting point. Obviously, if we used a metal that had a low melting point, we could not allow the electricity to heat it up enough to give a good light. Tungsten melts at 3,380 degrees Centigrade, but because surface evaporation takes place even below this point and would shorten the life of the lamp, the temperature is not allowed to rise much above 2,000 degrees. The inert gas used in " gas-filled " lamps is generally nitrogen mixed with argon, a " rare " gas of the atmosphere.

Carbon would make a good filament and was originally used because of its high melting point, but it disintegrates too easily at very high temperatures and is now used only for lamps likely to have rough treatment, when high lighting efficiency is unnecessary.

# WHAT MAKES YOU GET A "LUMP IN YOUR THROAT"?

I WONDER if you know what " emotion " is ? Well, it is a very overpowering " feeling," caused by some unusual happening such as getting a beautiful present unexpectedly.

Now, when you get a strong feeling like this, the natural thing would be to give vent to it by shouting, singing, laughing, or crying. But if others are about you, you will restrain your feelings, then you will get a sudden " spasm " or " lump in your throat ! "

# WHAT IS THE DIFFERENCE BETWEEN A FROG AND A TOAD?

[*Harold Bastin.*

THE COMMON FROG.

IT is first of all necessary to realise that they are really not distant relations, but very alike. Both begin life in the same way by being tadpoles. They are both "amphibians," which means creatures able to live on land and water, and in this they are like newts. Both go to sleep in the winter in some place where they will not be disturbed, and they need not wake up for food. But if you pick up a frog and a toad, you will see at once one difference ; the frog is smooth and hard to hold ; the toad has a rough surface, with a number of lumps like warts ; it is not a *very* beautiful creature, but it has not been fairly treated by poets. If you look at the legs of the toad you will find the hind limbs are smaller than the frog's ; the toad does not leap so far as the frog and does not need such long hind legs. The frog, also, is a better swimmer. If you look at their eggs, you will see the frog's are like a jelly ; we call them frog's spawn, and we can see them in springtime on ponds. The toad's eggs are in long, narrow strings, with two rows of eggs stuck together. The toad is a villainous-looking creature, but it does not deserve all the hard things said of it. It is no more poisonous than a frog, but it suffers because of its looks.

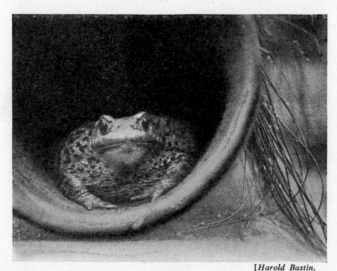

A TOAD.

[*Harold Bastin.*

61

# WHAT IS PHOSPHORESCENCE?

YOU know that the hands of a luminous watch will glow in the dark even though it is a long time since they were last " refreshed " by exposure to light. That is because they are phosphorescent, although there is a good deal of confusion as to the meaning of the term. In this sense almost all materials are phosphorescent. They have the power of storing up light and releasing it again after a greater or lesser period. Phosphorus, which gives its name to this night glow, behaves in the same sort of way for quite a different reason. There is no need for the phosphorus to have been exposed in advance to radiation of any kind. The glow is due to the emission of light as part of the " energy balance " of some chemical change. The phosphorus is, in fact, slowly burning although the temperature may be as low as the freezing point of water. But strange though it may seem, chemists have found great difficulty in deciding either exactly what happens or why it happens. All that can really be said is that this kind of glow is the exact opposite of what happens when a camera film is exposed. In the one case, light produces chemical changes ; in the other, light is produced by chemical change.

# WHY WE GET TIRED?

IN every position of our bodies except that of lying flat on our backs, some of our muscles are in use ; that is to say, are " contracted " in order to keep that position. Every movement we make is also caused by one or more muscles contracting. Movements may be gentle and slow or strong and quick, as in running, jumping and field games. All our muscles possess what is called " energy " or " power to act," and as more movements take place, this " energy " is gradually used up. If you walk twenty yards, you feel as fresh as when you started ; if you walk twenty miles, you " feel tired," because the " energy " is used up and your reason tells you that you have done enough. But not only " used " muscles make you " feel tired." Looking too long at a bright light, listening too long to musical sounds, or to the reading of a dull book, have the effect of tiring the nerves of sight and sound, and so you " feel tired."

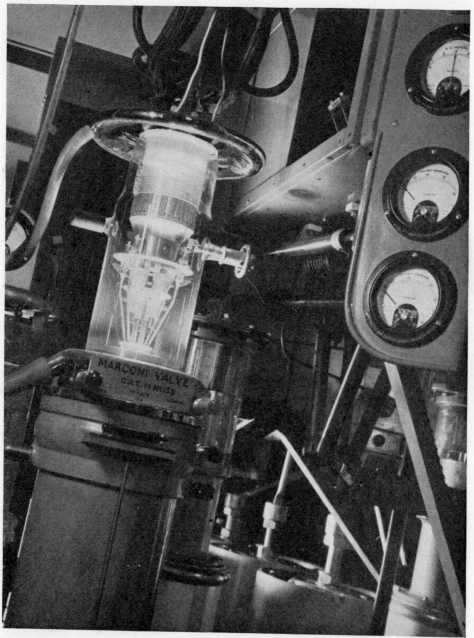

A LARGE TYPE OF HIGH-POWER WATER-COOLED VALVE USED AT THE
TRANSMITTING STATION AT DROITWICH.

SHEETS OF POSTAGE STAMPS SEEN COMING OFF A PRINTING MACHINE.

A DOG-SLEIGH AT THE BASE OF AN ICEBERG.

# HOW AN ICEBERG IS FORMED?

GLACIERS are very slow-moving rivers of ice which drain cold countries of their surplus snow just as the more familiar rivers of liquid water drain warmer countries like ours of their surplus rain. Where the glaciers of polar lands meet the sea, pieces break away during the annual spring and summer thaw and begin to drift away to the tropics. These broken-off pieces are icebergs. Most of the big icebergs which so endanger shipping in the north Atlantic Ocean are thus shed by the glaciers of Greenland, which is a country of practically nothing else but snowfields and glaciers. Icebergs from the vast Jacobshavn glacier (Greenland) have been known to tower six hundred feet and more above the sea surface. As eight-ninths of a floating iceberg are submerged and only one-ninth is above water and visible, the total height of these must have been *nearly a mile*, and their total weight over *one thousand million tons*. There is no mystery, therefore, as to how a great forty-thousand-ton Atlantic liner like the *Titanic* could be smashed and sunk by collision with an iceberg. The *Titanic* was big and heavy, but the iceberg

was probably as much as five thousand times heavier. A ship can
" scent " the approach of a big berg by thermometer readings. The
temperature of the sea may fall by three or four degrees F. in ten
or fifteen minutes. Eventually, of course, as they reach warmer
regions, icebergs melt away entirely.

[E.N.A.

**SEALS ASLEEP IN THE SHADOW OF A GIANT ICEBERG.**

A GOLDEN EAGLE IN FLIGHT.

[" *Topical* " *Press.*

# HOW A BIRD FLIES?

THERE is at least one kind of animal which really flies, the bat; there are some birds, for example, the ostrich, rhea, emu and cassowary, which do not fly but run. Speaking generally, however, birds are made to fly. It used to be thought that this power came from the fact that their bones are hollow and can be filled with air, or because they have little sacs filled with air all over the body. But today it is no longer thought that these sacs and air-filled bones make the bird able to fly. It is better to look at the way in which a bird is shaped. It looks like a boat with the breast-bone for a keel; and if we think of the air as in some way like the water, we shall see how this keel helps the bird. Air, of course, has much less resistance in it than water; but the bird in the air and the fish in the water have much in common. With its wings the bird propels itself through the air, and just as a boat has a rudder by means of which it is steered, so the bird uses the feathers of its tail to steer its course. It has been said that in proportion to its size, the wings of a bird are approximately two hundred and forty times more powerful than the arms of a man.

# WHY COLOURS LOOK DIFFERENT BY ARTIFICIAL LIGHT?

THE eye is a deceiver in many ways, but most of all in the judging of colour. But the fault is not altogether the eye's. The fact is that a tie or a blouse or a wallpaper has not any one colour. It merely has the property of absorbing all other wavelengths of light except those we recognise, taken together, as its colour. The colour we see is what is left when the tie or blouse or the wallpaper has taken its pick from all the varied wavelengths of light which happen to be falling upon it. What is left obviously depends on the character of the illumination. A " pure " red would, for example, look black if viewed in a blue light, and so would a pure blue in a red light. In neither case would any of the only colour which it was capable of reflecting be provided. In the same way, the greater yellowness of artificial light, as compared with sunlight, is quite sufficient to alter the " balance " of the light reflected from any object so illuminated.

# WHY ARE WE ABLE TO THINK AND REMEMBER?

THE brain is the great organ which receives and interprets impressions passed to it by the nerves of our five senses. It is made up of millions of tiny " brain cells," special " areas " devoted to receiving sensations from the " sense " organs and giving orders to our " moving " organs, the muscles ; and lastly, of a complicated system of communicating " fibres "—minute electric wires, as it were.

When a child is born, practically all the " cells " which have to do with " thinking " and " memory " contain innumerable little " granules," but have no " impressions."

Soon after birth, the senses begin to " take notice "—see, hear, feel, etc—and the impressions are passed to the brain cells and make what we call " experience."

As the years advance, the brain, by putting one experience with another, performs the act called " thinking," and when someone asks a question, or a particular sight, sound or smell is conveyed to the brain from these senses, it is able, by communication between its " cells," to recall other experiences—it " remembers."

# WHAT MAKES A BALL BOUNCE?

AIR, when it is compressed, naturally has a tendency to decompress and return to its natural state under the conditions of temperature and pressure. A rubber ball contains air, and when it is dropped with some force, the flexible rubber is pressed inwards and flattened, so that the air is compressed. As the rubber reaches

L.E.A.]                    BOUNCING A FOOTBALL.                    [H. Armstrong Roberts.

the limit of movement in accordance with the force exerted on it, it tends to spring back to its normal shape, which resists the air pressure evenly upon the inside surface. This tendency is increased by the pressure of the air inside seeking to return to its normal volume. Hence, the rubber is shot back and the force makes the ball return or " bounce." The amount a ball bounces for a given drop also depends upon the temperature and pressure of the air inside.

# WHAT IS THE ORIGIN OF A SUNDIAL?

IF you want to know the time nowadays, you can look at your watch or the nearest clock, or listen-in to the wireless signal. In olden days, however, man had no means of telling the exact hour.

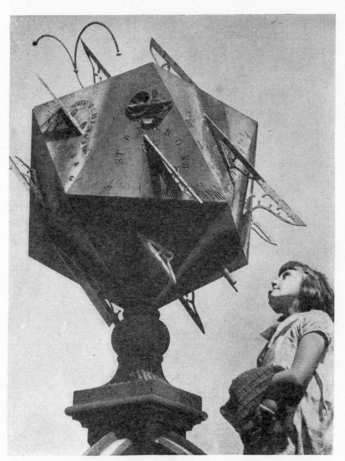

[Fox Photos, Ltd.

THIS UNUSUAL SUNDIAL TELLS THE TIME OF ALL THE CHIEF CITIES OF THE WORLD.

He could reckon only on three definite moments : firstly, at sunrise ; secondly, when the sun was highest in the sky; and thirdly, at sunset. Later on, the earliest form of " time-piece "— the sundial — was invented. The Greeks were probably among the first to use one, and Herodotus the historian tells us that they were indebted to the Babylonians for the idea underlying it. You will find a reference to one in the book of Isaiah, where we read of " the sundial of Ahaz " (B.C. 713). A sundial shows the time of day by means of a shadow cast by an upright rod, called a gnomon, on a flat plate, or dial, on which the twelve hours are marked. Specimens are to be seen still on the walls of churches, or fixed on pillars in old-fashioned gardens. A great disadvantage of the sundial, of course, is that it gives no information unless the sun is shining. This drawback is referred to in the motto which was often engraved on the dial—" I mark only the bright hours."

# HOW A SODA-WATER SYPHON WORKS?

A SODA-WATER syphon is filled at the mineral water works with soda-water and carbonic acid gas under pressure. The neck of the syphon is fitted with a valve A, which has a head B fitting up against a seating C. Below the seating is a glass tube D, which extends to nearly the bottom of the syphon bottle.

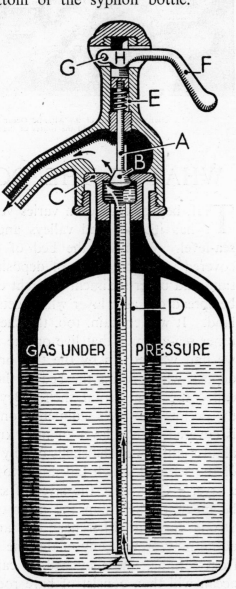

The pressure of the gas liberated from the soda-water (which still retains a large amount) above the surface of the water forces the water up the tube and presses the valve B on its seat, the valve being also kept there by the spring E.

The valve can be pressed down, against the pressure of the gas and the spring E, by a hand-lever F, which extends outside the head of the syphon. It is pivoted at G, so when pressure is put on the thumb-piece of the lever, pressing at H against the top of the valve A, it moves it down off its seat, and the soda-water is forced up the tube D by the gas and expelled. This is clearly shown in the diagram by the arrows, out of the spout of the syphon.

There is sufficient compressed gas in the syphon to force the water out till its level falls to the bottom end of the tube D, when the remaining gas is spluttered out.

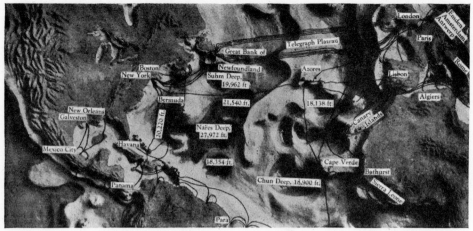

A chart of the bed of the Atlantic Ocean, showing its hills, valleys, and mountains
and the routes of the various ocean cables.

# WHAT IS THE OCEAN BED LIKE?

THE bed of the ocean varies very much from place to place and
has its hills and valleys and mountains like the land above
sea-level. Wherever the bed of the ocean is level enough, it is
covered with some sort of deposit. Near the land this will be of
sand and other sediment brought down to the sea by rivers and will
be spread out as a layer which gets thinner and finer away from the
land. It will contain, too, the shells and skeletons of shell-fish and
other sea-animals that live on the rock and in the shallows, such as
we find washed up by the tide on the shore. This is the kind of
deposit which forms the bed of the ocean near the land on what is
called the Continental shelf. Beyond this, in the deeper parts of
the oceans to which sediment from the land is not carried, the bed
is covered with a layer of mud known as ooze, which is made up
almost entirely of the shells of tiny animals that live near the surface
of the sea and which fall down to the bottom as they die, forming
a layer. Of course, the layer of sand and mud near the shore will
be much thicker than the layer of ooze made in the same time.
Strong currents either near the land or in the deeper parts of the
ocean may prevent any of the fine mud or the small animal remains
from settling, and they will be carried elsewhere ; the bed of the
ocean will then consist of bare rock.

# WHERE CORK COMES FROM ?

WE may see cork being formed almost any time when out of doors. Wounds are as dangerous to plants as they are to animals, and when a caterpillar in feeding injures a leaf, it exposes the internal plant tissues to bacterial and fungal attacks.

Almost immediately the antiseptic is applied. From a tissue within the plant, called callus, new cells are formed to close the wounded parts. These cells quickly become brown, and assume the nature of true cork. In a like manner we see young green stems, and buds, change to a brown colour, a layer of cork tissues being formed outside to retain the moisture within.

Man, taking his cue from Nature, likewise finds cork useful to preserve liquids. He, however, requires it in comparatively large supplies. Consequently, he seeks for a species of tree that produces it in quantity.

In parts of Southern France, Spain, and in the forests of Algeria, he finds the Cork Oak (*Quercus suber*), the outer bark consists largely of cork. This is peeled off in wide strips during the summer season, done skilfully so that it does not injure the tree, but only tends to encourage it to form new layers to replace those removed. It is these layers that provide the corks for bottles and mats for bathrooms.

STRIPPING CORK TREES. [E.N.A.

73

# WHAT BIRDS CAN WALK ON THE SURFACE OF THE WATER?

THE Jacana, which is sometimes called the Water-pheasant, gets its name from Brazil ; its home is in the tropics, but it may be found also in Australia. It used to be classed with the water-hens, but now the family has a name of its own, the *Parridae*. It has long, thin legs but the most striking thing about it is the length of its toes. These long toes make it able to move across the surface of a lake. It does not walk on the water itself, but it uses the water-lilies and aquatic plants as stepping-stones or as a kind of bridge.

The Jacana is related to the Rails. It makes its nest on the water, in a tiny island of grass, or in reeds, and there it lays its olive-green eggs. We can picture this bird as always at home in some lake, covered with large water-lilies, in India or Ceylon, Brazil or Australia.

It is easy to see in our picture how its long toes enable it to walk from lily to lily. By their means the bird can distribute its weight evenly over a wide area, just as a traveller over the snow uses huge snowshoes to spread out his weight.

[*E.N.A.*

A Brazilian Jacana walking on the surface of a pond, using the leaves of water lilies and other aquatic plants as stepping-stones.

PELICANS AT THEIR TOILET.    [*P. G. Luck.*

# TELL ME, PLEASE ?

1. What is St. Elmo's fire?
2. What were called the Pillars of Hercules?
3. What is meant by Erse?
4. What is an okapi?
5. Who was the Egyptian Sun God?
6. How are an alligator's eggs hatched?
7. What is a gnu?
8. What is copra?
9. What is a scarab?
10. What is an assegai?
11. What is the origin of the term " Thumbs up " ?
12. What do we mean by *pons asinorum*?
13. What is the Blarney Stone?
14. What birds do the Chinese train to catch fish?

*For answers to these questions see page* 76.

# ANSWERS TO QUESTIONS on page 75

1. An electrical phenomenon that causes the tops of masts of ships at sea to glow.

2. An ancient name for the rocks, Calpe in Europe, or Gibraltar as we know it, and Abyla, or Ceuta, in Africa, marking the entrance to the Mediterranean Sea.

3. The Irish and Gaelic languages.

4. An African animal somewhat like a giraffe, but with a shorter neck.

5. Ra.

6. By the sun's heat on the sand in which they are laid.

7. An African antelope.

8. Dried coconut.

9. A sacred Egyptian beetle.

10. A slender Zulu spear of hard wood.

11. The crowds at the Roman arenas made this gesture when they desired that the life of a fallen gladiator should be spared—an expression now meaning " in luck's way."

12. A proposition expounded by Euclid.

13. A stone set in the wall of Castle Blarney, near Cork, Ireland, and difficult of access. It is said that anyone who kisses the Blarney Stone is endowed with heroic powers of cajolery or persuasion.

14. Cormorants.

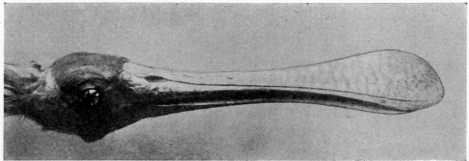

[H. Bastin.

### THE HEAD OF A SPOONBILL.

This bill is called a " spatulate " type, and it enables the bird, which derives its name from this useful organ, to forage in the mud for its food.

A RAZORBILL. [*R. Thompson.*]

# WHY BIRDS HAVE BEAKS?

WHEN we compare ourselves with other living creatures, we at once see how much we do with our hands. Indeed, man owes his mastery over other creatures to such little things as these ; he has a hand and especially a thumb. Birds, however, though they have nothing like our hands, have their beaks, and it is remarkable what they can do with them. They find their food by means of their beaks ; and those which are birds of prey, hawks and eagles, for example, have beaks curved in such a way that they can fasten upon their living victims. Birds are provided with beaks of different shapes and sizes for a variety of purposes ; the pelican uses its large beak to catch fish, the woodpecker its narrow, pointed beak to penetrate bark and wood in its search for insects, while the tailor-bird sews together leaves to form a nest. If they make their nests under the ground, like the kingfisher, the beak acts like a spade to make a hole. The beak has to be made very strong for all these many tasks ; since it is the only tool which the bird has, it is surrounded by a horny or leathery covering. Everything depends upon the beak, it would not do for it to be easily put out of action. Besides its other uses, the beak is a weapon of war when birds go out to fight.

# HOW FAST THE EARTH ROTATES AT THE EQUATOR AND AT THE POLES?

THE earth rotates with a speed of about one thousand and thirty miles an hour at the equator, while at the poles it does not rotate at all. This is for the same reason that the outermost ring of hobby-horses on a merry-go-round travel fastest, while the central point of the rod or pivot round which the merry-go-round revolves does not

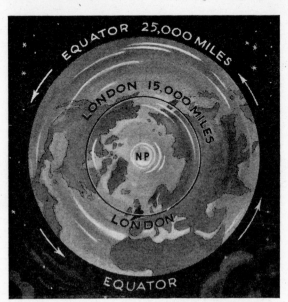

move at all. The north and south poles represent the top and bottom of the great imaginary rod, or axis, round which the merry-go-round earth spins. The equator, as it were, represents the outermost ring of hobby-horses and it measures nearly twenty-five thousand miles around. People living in different latitudes are like children riding on different rings of horses. If we live in London, we ride upon a smaller ring, an inner ring measuring only about fifteen thousand five hundred miles around. As the earth turns round once in twenty-four hours, Londoners travel at only six hundred and fifty miles an hour, for they have only fifteen thousand five hundred miles to cover in the twenty-four hours, whereas equator-dwellers must move at one thousand and thirty miles an hour.

# WHY WE WINK?

THE *common* habit we all have of "winking" every few seconds or minutes is done, not by an effort of the will, but "involuntarily"—that is, by a reflex act, not by thinking. The surface of the eye is sensitive to dust and draughts, and it *must* be kept *moist*. Invisible tears keep it moist, and the rapid "winking" of the eyelids "sweeps" the moisture and the dust towards two tiny holes on the inner corners of the lids, whence it runs into the nose.

# HOW IS ICE MADE?

YOU know that even warm water feels cool if we wait for it to dry off of its own accord. That is because heat is necessary to transform water into water vapour, even if the change takes place at quite an ordinary temperature instead of at boiling point, as in the case of a kettle. When we perspire on a hot day, it means that our body is trying to cool itself by evaporation, and when we want to make ice, we use the same property of another liquid. What is required is obviously a liquid which can be conveniently vaporised at temperatures at least down to the freezing point of water.

Ammonia, which is the " smell " of smelling salts, is the one normally used. A refrigerator is simply a machine in which ammonia is alternately evaporated and condensed again to a liquid. Evaporation is caused by a sudden expansion of the ammonia, and condensation by an increase in pressure. In ice-making, the ammonia, cooled by evaporation, is passed through a series of pipes, round which the water freezes. It then passes back to the machine to be used over again, so that quite a small amount of ammonia can be used to make an almost indefinite amount of ice.

STORING FISH IN AN ICE REFRIGERATOR.

# HOW IS STEEL MADE STAINLESS?

STAINLESS steel, as distinct from chromium-plated steel, is, like all steels, an alloy in which iron, carbon, nitrogen, cobalt, or some other metal is present. The "stainless" quality is due to the fact that the surface is protected by a thin "self-healing" film of oxygen. The film is so thin that it can be detected only by X-rays, probably fifty thousand times thinner than the paper of this page. The minute percentage of chromium in the iron is responsible for making the steel stainless, but stainless steel was invented and used long before it was understood why it was stainless. About eighteen per cent. chromium and eight per cent. nickel is found in most stainless steels, although the exact proportion varies according to the other qualities, such as the toughness or tensile strength which is required.

# WHY A BOOMERANG RETURNS TO THE THROWER?

THE boomerang, which is used by the aborigines, or natives, of certain parts of Australia, is a wonderfully effective weapon when thrown with skill. It is a curved blade of hard wood weighing about half-a-pound, from two to three feet in length, generally quite flat on one side and slightly convex on the other. The name "boomerang," which is a native word, would lead one to expect that it booms when travelling through the air, but it makes rather a whistling noise.

There are two kinds of boomerang, one which does *not* return to the sender when thrown—and this variety is used in war, but it is the other sort we think of when we speak of a "boomerang flight." These hunting boomerangs are thrown with a peculiar twist and, after describing a circle, come back to the thrower. This is due to the shape of the weapon, one arm of which offers more resistance to the air than the other portion, causing it to travel in a curved path after it has slowed down below a certain rate of speed.

A skilled thrower has been known to make his boomerang travel more than two hundred yards, and even to cause it to return to him after striking the ground, but in the ordinary way, if the object aimed at is hit, the weapon does not fly back. It can accomplish this only after a clear flight.

# WHAT TOAD CARRIES ITS YOUNG ON ITS BACK?

WE know that the frogs and toads in our ponds set free their eggs, which float on the water. That is the general way of these half-and-half creatures which live on both water and land—*amphibians* is their correct name. One strange kind of toad is called the *Surinam*, and makes its home in Guiana and Brazil. The skin on the back of the female Surinam toad is full of small holes. Somehow she manages, probably with the help of the father toad, to get the eggs upon her back. There they sink into these holes like cradles, and the holes are then closed. Soon, from the eggs come the little toads. Though they are not able to wag their tails in the water as other tadpoles do, they go through a similar stage while they are still lodged on their mother's back. There they live till they are fully grown and can begin life on their own account. It is said that there may be from sixty to a hundred eggs, and they may lie three months on the back of the mother. The Surinam is not a beautiful toad; it has very large hind legs, its back looks very rough. It is, none the less, a wonderful creature to have a back which serves as a nursery for a large family for so long.

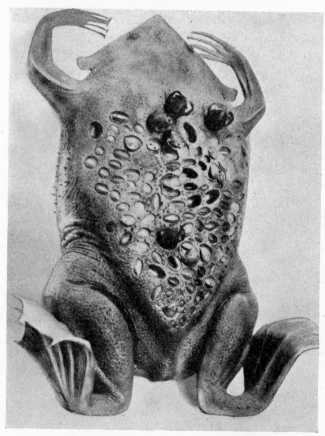

[*Sport & General.*

A FEMALE SURINAM TOAD, WITH EGGS AND YOUNG ON ITS BACK.

# WHY WE FEEL PAIN?

THE whole of our body is covered with skin, and beneath its outermost layer are millions of nerve endings, so close together that a pin-point cannot touch *any* part without causing a sensation of " touch," " pain," or " agony "—according to the lightness or depth of the prick.

Other little nerve points, not quite so close together, give us the sensation of " heat " or " cold ", which, if exaggerated, causes " pain " also. The skin, therefore, is the organ of " touch " and is our contact with the world outside ourselves.

The *cause* of pain is injury, inflammation, or disease affecting these nerves of " feeling ". WHY we feel " pain " is because the brain, which judges of the place and character of the sensation, tells us that something is wrong and warns us to take measures to put it right. People often say, " They hate pain, it is so cruel " ; and so it may be ; but more often it is a kindly warning by Nature, so that, if we take notice of the " pain " this time, we may learn how to avoid it another. Or, if it is an " internal pain," it may tell a doctor exactly what is wrong with us.

# WHERE MISTLETOE GROWS?

THE mistletoe is most familiar on the apple tree, but it may less frequently be found on other trees botanically allied, as the hawthorn, wild service tree, mountain ash, and, much more rarely, the pear. Next to the apple, the black poplar is the tree that it most prefers as its host, but it may select the lime, sycamore, maple, silver fir, larch and various pines. It is but rarely found on the oak. A careful inquiry once made in that connection, produced only seven authentic instances in all England of oaks on which mistletoe was found.

Our British Christmas supplies come chiefly from the Hertfordshire apple orchards, the Welsh border, and the West of England. Many tons come in from abroad, largely from Brittany.

Although the mistletoe is especially abundant in the West of England, yet it does not extend to Cornwall. Yorkshire is about its northern limit, and it is not found in either Scotland or Ireland.

GATHERING MISTLETOE FOR CHRISTMAS.

# WHY WE SEE OUR BREATH IN COLD WEATHER?

WE can see our breath on a cold day because, like the air in a house for tropical plants, it is both warm and damp. Air can hold only a certain amount of water vapour at a given temperature. The hotter it is, the more it can hold. That is why, although a bathing-dress will dry quickly on a hot day, the same air that has absorbed moisture from the bathing-dress will throw it down again as dew during the night. In the same way, our breath, when we breathe it out, is quite warm enough to hold all the moisture we have given it. But if it is very cold outside, some of the moisture immediately condenses into a miniature fog.

# HOW IS A LOCOMOTIVE'S POWER AND SPEED TESTED?

THE power of a locomotive, for practical purposes, is tested by a " draw bar pull," that is, the force it can exert in pulling the rest of the train—the tender and coaches—is recorded.

This can be done with the engine stationary by the device shown in the illustration. The photograph shows a Western Region engine

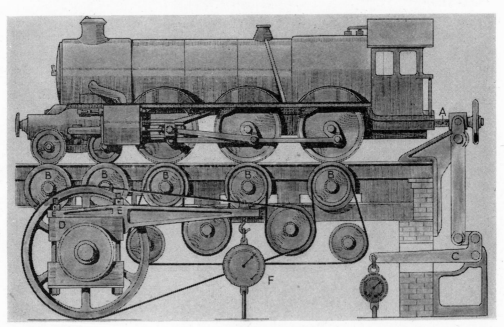

# HOW ARE LOCOMOTIVES TESTED ?

[*Fox Photos.*

**A WESTERN REGION LOCOMOTIVE UNDERGOING A TEST ON THE PLANT AT SWINDON.**

being tested in the locomotive shop at Swindon. The diagram demonstrates, in modified form, how the engine is held by the draw bar A so that it cannot move forward off the wheels B on which it stands. As the throttle is opened, the engine begins to rotate these wheels, which are mounted so that each wheel or roller can be arranged to come under a wheel of the engine, the whole weight of which is on the rollers instead of on the rails. The draw bar of the engine is coupled to a steelyard or weighing machine C and the pull is read on the scale F (as would be a weight being weighed) in tons. Resistance is offered to the rotation of the rollers (which are all coupled by belts) by a big drum brake D, the pressure of which, by tightening the nuts E, can be increased to represent the train load, so that all the conditions of actual operation can be obtained with the engine itself at rest.

# WHY WATER BUBBLES WHEN BOILED?

WHEN you fill a kettle with water and put it on the gas till it boils, you will see bubbles rising to the surface. These are due to the fact that, when the gas makes the kettle hot, the heat makes the air in the water expand and the air escapes to the top in bubbles. These bubbles are simply envelopes of water with the air inside. Since the gas begins to make the water at the bottom of the kettle hot first, it is there the envelopes with the hot air are first made; then they rise till you see the surface of the water one mass of bubbles.

# WHY BIRDS SING?

IT is not hard to tell how the sound comes from the bird. It has a most delicate organ in the larynx, through which the music comes. But what makes it sing? We know that it is the song of the bird to his mate. Birds also call to each other when they want their friends to rally round, for many kinds of birds delight to be together in flocks. But it is scarcely possible to find a suitable explanation for the songs of the lark which we hear on a lovely spring day. Perhaps, as poets have said, they sing simply because, being happy, they can't help it.

THE NIGHTINGALE.    [Reginald Gaze.

[*Keystone*

AN OASIS IN THE SAHARA DESERT.

# TELL ME, PLEASE?

1. What do we mean by an oasis?

2. For what does P.S. stand?

3. On what occasion does a judge don a black cap?

4. Which legs does a cow use first when getting up?

5. What is a heifer?

6. What do we say when we mean a number of : (*a*) partridges, (*b*) geese, (*c*) wild ducks, (*d*) cows, (*e*) sheep, (*f*) fish, (*g*) puppies, (*h*) bees?

7. What jewel do the superstitious consider unlucky?

8. If salt is upset at table, how do superstitious people say bad luck can be averted?

9. What sign does a pawnbroker display?

10. What sign does a barber display?

11. With what city do you associate the word " gondola "?

12. What do we call a female fox?

*For answers to these questions see page 88.*

# ANSWERS TO QUESTIONS on page 87

1. An isolated spring of water, surrounded by vegetation, found in the desert.
2. Post scriptum, meaning " written afterwards."
3. When passing sentence of death.
4. The hind legs.
5. A young cow.
6. (*a*) covey, (*b*) gaggle, (*c*) flight, (*d*) herd, (*e*) flock, (*f*) shoal, (*g*) litter, (*h*) swarm.
7. The opal.
8. By throwing a pinch of it over the left shoulder.
9. Three golden balls.
10. A striped pole.
11. Venice.
12. Vixen.

[*British Railways.*

TIGHTENING STAYS AT A FIREBOX.
A scene from the Boiler Shop of the B.R. Locomotive Depot at Swindon.

# WHY CINEMA FIGURES APPEAR TO MOVE?

THE human eye is a camera, but it cannot receive and interpret more than a certain number of "snapshots" a second. If a great number of images are presented to it, they become blended together and the result may be a blur. The spokes of a rapidly - revolving wheel, for instance, appear as a solid sheet.

TECHNICIANS EXAMINING A FILM STRIP.

In the cinema, a number of images, usually twenty-two a second, are projected on the screen, each giving a separate picture of some movement. The twenty-two pictures of a man lifting his leg off the ground, for instance, would show first his leg on the ground, then his leg half an inch up, then his leg an inch up, and so on. Each is a separate picture, but projected on the screen rapidly, it appears as if we were actually watching a continuous picture of the leg being lifted, instead of twenty-two separate pictures. The eye " retains " the vision of the last picture just long enough to blend it with the next.

Now you may ask why the picture is not blurred as it is with the spokes of a wheel. The answer is that a shutter is used which completely shuts off all light for a minute fraction of a second between each picture. The period when the screen is actually blank is too short to be appreciated by the eye, but it is important because it allows the pictures to be blended without blurring. If a film were projected much slower than twenty-two pictures a second, we should see the figures jerking. " Slow motion " is actually fast motion, many more than twenty-two pictures a second being taken by the camera and then presented more slowly to the audience.

[*Mirrorpic.*

SOME EVER-MOVING DUNES OF SAND ARE A HUNDRED FEET HIGH.

# WHAT IS A DESERT?

A DESERT is a dry region where, because there is practically no rain, there is no vegetation and the surface of the land is bare. Deserts are usually situated in the centre of the larger masses of land like Australia, Africa and Asia, and are cut off from the sea by mountain ranges. Most of the winds that blow from the big land masses are dry winds, while the damp winds from the sea are robbed of their moisture before they have reached the interior of the continent. Sea winds will quickly lose their moisture if they have to pass over high mountains near the coast. Most of the big deserts like the Sahara in Africa, the Gobi in Asia, Central Australia, as well as others in North and South America, are either near the centre of large land masses or are protected from the moist sea breezes by high mountains near the coast.

When a land surface is free from vegetation, the sun has great power during the day, and the nights are very cold. This causes the rocks to crack and break up, while the wind wears the smaller pieces down to sand. Thus deserts, as well as being without vegetation, are generally stony and sandy.

THE PYRAMID OF KHEFREN.

This pyramid retains, near the top, a portion of the original casing of polished stone.

# HOW ARE THINGS ELECTRO-PLATED?

THE secret of electro-plating lies in the chemist's test-tube. Everyone who has performed any chemical experiments knows that in a test-tube things happen very quickly. Litmus changes instantaneously from blue to red or *vice versa*, and almost all the colours of the rainbow can be produced or destroyed at will. This is because nearly all chemicals are split up, when dissolved in water, into two parts, one part carrying a positive electrical charge and the other a negative charge. This preliminary splitting-up enormously accelerates chemical changes. It is also the basis of electro-plating; for, when an electric current is passed through a solution of a metallic salt, the metal and acid parts of the salt are driven to the two terminals. All that is necessary, therefore, is to use the object to be plated as one terminal, to provide salt containing the right metal, and to pass the current in the right direction for the second metal to be deposited on the first. It is not, however, so easy a job for an amateur to undertake as it might at first appear. The salt must be of the right concentration, and the rate of current-flow must be nicely controlled if perfect electro-plating is to be secured.

# HOW YOU SPEAK?

SPEECH is the expression of your thoughts or intentions by sounds. You can speak in the ordinary way, or sing, or you can whisper. When you *whisper*, you make different sounds with your lips, teeth, tongue, and mouth while breathing out. When you *talk* or *sing*, you use the same parts, but first make a musical sound by vibrating your " vocal cords ". These cords are two thin tapes of a white elastic structure placed parallel with each other in the " voice-box," half-way down your throat. When the breath passes between them, you can, by tightening, slackening, bringing them together or separating them, produce almost as many notes as a piano. As the chosen note passes through the mouth, you modify it by the parts named above. If you say the alphabet slowly to your-self, you will understand. In A, your tongue presses the bottom teeth and you open your mouth; in B, your lips come together and separate quickly; in C, your teeth come together and separate quickly—and so on. Then you learn, by putting letters together, to sound " words ", and later, words together to make sentences.

# WHAT IS AN ARTESIAN WELL?

THE first well of this kind in Europe was sunk at Artois, in northern France, in 1126. Hence the name "Artesian." A hole is driven down perpendicularly into the ground till it reaches a layer of water under pressure, which then rises up in the well. It is, of course, only in certain localities, where the geological structure of the district and the substratum is such as to cause water to accumulate there under pressure, that such a well is practicable. In alluvial soil (water-borne matter deposited through the ages) boring is by connected rods and special boring tools, but in chalk, sandstone and strata other than solid rock, also in deep borings of three hundred to four hundred feet, a cable percussion system is used, a winch lifting the tool and suddenly dropping it.

*By courtesy of]*    *[G. Richards & Co.*
LOWERING A ROD.

The rods are lowered as shown in our photograph, and are rotated as they are forced or dumped downwards by their weight till water is reached. In harder formations such as solid limestone, granite and similar rocks, tubular drills are used, and these cut out a core of the substance (like an apple core) by rotation.

If the ground is soft, and might collapse, tubes are forced down around the drill as boring proceeds and make a permanent pipe. A clay auger is used in such cases and is rotated by three or four men, the clay being brought up inside the auger by cable and winch. In sandstone special chisels are used, hoisted by the winch and dropped repeatedly. The debris is brought up from time to time by a "sludge" or "dipper" which has a non-return valve in the lower end; so holding the debris and allowing it to be drawn up by the winch.

Petroleum too, is tapped by means of Artesian wells, as described in our article: *How do we get Oil from the Earth,* page 58.

[*Will F. Taylor.*

SILVER BIRCHES IN SHERWOOD FOREST.

# CAN YOU NAME THAT TREE?

TO recognize the various trees one does not have to be in a hurry. A few observations of details are well worth while.

Each tree has its own distinctive characters, and with a little effort these are easily fixed in the mind.

A simple method is, during winter, to mark out a few trees and carefully note the formation of their branches against the sky. Then enter in your notebook what you think them to be. Afterwards carefully watch those trees as they develop, and check off your errors.

Probably the first development will be flowers on the bare branches. In the case of the common elm, they will be on the topmost branches, and rooks, while building their nests, will often oblige by dropping a specimen branch.

The little clusters of reddish elm flowers gradually change to groups of leaf-like fruits with a swollen seed near their upper end, and these, when ripe, fall to the ground like confetti.

While making your observation of the common elm flowers, you may discover another tree producing almost the same kind of blooms, but with much more spreading branches. Eventually, this

94

A FINE BEECH TREE—DEFACED BY THOUGHTLESS PEOPLE.

second tree ripens its fruits, which are again leaf-like and similar to those of the common elm, but their seeds are much more centrally placed on the leafy appendage. By these details you have incidentally identified the wych elm, as well as the species you set out to observe.

Such details any good botanical work will assist to verify, and new discoveries will continually occur as the season advances.

The ash also has brownish flowers on bare branches, but these change to winged seeds, or

Male and bud-like female catkins of the hazel tree.

" keys ", one propeller to each seed. Presently, though, we are finding similar winged seeds but in pairs. Look then at the foliage. In the ash with the one-propeller fruits, the leaves consist of seven to eleven leaflets, but those of the tree with the two-propeller fruits are large and five-lobed. That feature, together with the paired fruits, show it to be the sycamore.

Having identified the sycamore's leaf, it is easy to go astray should you afterwards meet with a plane tree with similarly shaped leaves. A glance at its fruits will, however, show them as a pendulous globular collection of small seeds without any winged propellers.

The various tree barks should also be observed, smooth in the beech, rugged in the oak and elm, white and silvery in the birch.

Photos]                          [J. J. Ward.

Elm flowers, which appear on the topmost branches and before the leaves.

The Redskin folk like colourful decoration and a bold pattern adorns the pack in which this Indian baby—the papoose—travels comfortably on his mother's back.

TRICK RIDERS DEMONSTRATING THEIR SKILL AND DARING.

# WHY WE GET SUNBURNT?

"SUNLIGHT" consists of a number of different rays, and not simply of the white light by which we see. The rays which cause sunburn are the ultra-violet, and they have a very much shorter wavelength than white light rays. Because they are shorter, they penetrate the skin surface and act on the cells beneath. The benefits to health which results from laying in the sun is really a chemical action, and arises from ultra-violet light producing vitamin D which is so important to the growth of bones and teeth. The actual change in colour is caused by the formation of melanin, or brown pigment, in the skin, which serves to a certain extent as a protection against an overdose.

[*Topical Press.*

RABBITS ENJOYING AN ARTIFICIAL SUN-BATH.

# HAVE YOU SEEN RED SNOW?

CERTAINLY you have never seen "red" snow in England, but in other parts of the world—on mountains in South Europe and also in Greenland—snow of a reddish or greenish hue falls sometimes. The colour is caused by the presence of a very tiny organism present in the air, called *Protococcus nivalis*. Occasionally a "yellow" snow has been found, and in this case the coloration has been shown to be due to minute particles of pollen from pine trees. Have you ever wondered why ordinary snow should be *white*? This is because the light is reflected from the countless surfaces of the snow crystals.

Another instance of strange colouring is found in the Antarctic, where the ice has a yellowish-brown tint due to a layer of tiny vegetable organisms called diatoms. As the coats of the polar bears in winter turn a light yellowish shade, they are less visible against this surface, and here we have a good example of what is known as "protective colouring."

# WHAT IS AN OAK APPLE?

THE oak apple is not a fruit. It is an abnormal growth produced on the oak by a minute gall-wasp.

[J. J. Ward.

AN OAK APPLE JUST BEFORE THE GALL-WASPS EMERGE FROM IT.

This tiny, wingless insect comes out of the ground during the month of December to lay its eggs inside the oak buds. The oak apple then forms around the eggs, and in June numerous holes appear about it, from which emerge tiny, winged gall-wasps. These wasps then burrow into the ground and lay their eggs on the roots of the oak, where other galls then begin to form.

From the root galls come the wingless gall-wasps, which appear in winter, and crawl up to the buds to deposit their eggs and so repeat the process.

[*Topical.*

A WATERSPOUT AT SEA.

# WHAT IS A WATERSPOUT?

A WATERSPOUT is a kind of little brother to a tornado or cyclone or typhoon, and all these are in the nature of violent whirlwinds or revolving storms. When certain atmospheric conditions are fulfilled, water from a rain-cloud descends, not in separate drops, but as a continuous rotating column or spout which looks like a mammoth, ragged rope connecting the earth and sky. It generally swoops down like a " bolt from the blue," only it is not from the blue but from the ominous blackness of a low-hanging thundercloud. The column, or spout, itself travels at anything up to fifty miles an hour over land or sea, while the water and air-currents in the column may revolve far faster. A frightful roar is usually made by the rapidly-whirling wind and water.

Waterspouts are commonest near the equator, but also occur in the temperate zone in spring and summer. Broadly speaking, they are caused, as also are American tornadoes, by the meeting of cool, dry currents of air with very much warmer, moister ones. The most effective mixing agency is a rotatory motion. The best way of mixing milk into a cup of tea is to stir them together. Nature stirs or whirls round opposing air currents as the best means of mixing them and restoring the balance of temperature and pressure.

# HOW AN AUTOMATIC WEIGHING MACHINE WORKS?

THE automatic weighing machine on which you take your weight after inserting a penny, consists of two or three distinct pieces of machinery. The first is concerned with your penny, which, when it is inserted, either by weight or by pressure releases a spring and allows the weighing mechanism to act. This device is made so that only a penny will be accepted and a badly-worn coin is rejected.

The actual weighing is carried out by means of a pendulum to which is attached a pointer working through a cam to limit the angle of rotation. The pressure downwards of your body makes the pendulum swing and this shows by the pointer swinging round the scale or by the delivery of a ticket or by the speaking of the weight.

The printing mechanism is quite simple, a number of weights in stones and pounds being set up on a mechanism through which passes a continuous strip of paper. When the pendulum registers the weight, the appropriate set of figures is brought to bear against the paper, which is then moved forward, cut neatly off and then delivered.

Similarly, the speaking device found on some machines is worked by the pendulum bringing a certain strip of sound film or gramophone record into position and actuating the reproducing mechanism as in an ordinary talking machine or gramophone.

# WHY A KETTLE SINGS?

A KETTLE sings because it is not boiling. Some minutes before the kettle boils, bubbles of steam begin to form at the bottom of the kettle where heat is being applied. But, although the first bubbles make a brave attempt to rise to the surface and escape as steam, they do not succeed in getting there. They are condensed back to water on the way.

The condensation of each bubble represents a miniature explosion in the water. All the explosions together make up the kettle's " sing." Naturally, when the kettle boils it stops singing. The bubbles then come straight through to the surface.

# WHAT IS AN AVALANCHE?

IN high mountains snow always falls instead of rain, and it accumulates to a considerable depth on the mountain slopes. Above the snow-line, where the snow practically never thaws and attains a great thickness, its weight presses it into ice, and it moves slowly down to lower ground as a glacier or an ice-sheet. Where, however, the slope on which the snow falls is very smooth and steep, or where there is thawing, the weight of the snow causes it to slip suddenly and rush down the mountain-side, carrying masses of rock, stones and everything in its way before it. In high mountains such as the Alps and the Himalayas, the warmth of the sun on the southern and western slopes will often cause an avalanche.

[Keystone.

MANY AVALANCHES OCCUR IN THE SWISS ALPS WHERE THESE TWO CHILDREN ARE LEARNING TO SKI.

# WHY ARE SOME EGGS COLOURED AND MARKED?

BEFORE we consider why eggs are coloured and marked, it is perhaps well to think of eggs without colour. Those of the green woodpecker, sand martin, kingfisher, and various owls offer examples of that kind.

These white eggs are found in underground burrows, or in the dark interior of trees, which seems to show that white eggs need concealment, or that white is the best colour for the parent birds to see their eggs in such dark places.

By courtesy of]      [The High Commissioner for New Zealand.
A CHAFFINCH'S NEST AND EGGS.

We sometimes find white, or pale-coloured, eggs in exposed nests, they are generally hidden by leaves, etc.

Eggs exposed on the ground, such as those of the night-jar and the plovers, are, on the contrary, usually marked to resemble the ground on which they are found, and are very inconspicuous. Similarly, the eggs of terns and other sea-birds laid on the shingle show a remarkable resemblance to the pebbles and sand.

On the other hand, the guillemot's egg, laid on a ledge of the bare cliff, may be almost any colour from pure white to a deep greenish-blue, with scribblings and blotches of various browns which seem to contradict the suggestion of protective coloration.

However, we should remember that the situation of the guillemot's eggs on almost inaccessible cliffs presents a different proposition.

What we have to bear in mind is the meaning these colours and markings may have to the particular natural enemies likely to attack the eggs. If, as is probable, few or no enemies seek the guillemot's eggs, there is no need for any regular colour scheme—which may account for such amazing variety.

# HOW A CARBURETTOR WORKS?

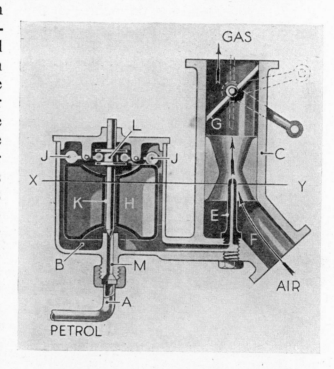

THE diagram shows how a carburettor mixes petrol and air to form an explosive gas mixture for a car or motor cycle engine. The petrol flows from the tank to the carburettor by a pipe A. It enters the float chamber B and passes along to the mixing chamber C and rises in the jet E. It does not flow out of the jet because the float mechanism in the chamber B controls its level at the dotted line X-Y.

The engine draws in air through the opening F when the throttle G is open (dotted lines show it open). The drawing in of the air forms a partial vacuum and causes petrol to spurt from the jet, mix with the up-going air and form an explosive gas for the engine. To prevent petrol from flowing out of the jet till the engine sucks it, there is a hollow float H in the float chamber B. When the level of the petrol rises, the float rises, pushes up the outer ends of the levers JJ, and their inner ends push down the needle K by the collar L, and so close the opening for the petrol at M. Opening or closing the throttle G regulates the power and speed of the engine.

# DO ANIMALS MIMIC ONE ANOTHER?

THERE are certain living creatures which cannot defend themselves and are liable to be eaten by their enemies. But near to them there are others which are so well able to take care of themselves, or are so horrid to taste, that these same enemies let them alone. Why should not the poor, defenceless creatures look like the others, so as to escape? More often than not they belong to the same group. There is the Golden Oriole, for example, in the Malayan Islands; in those same islands are the Friar-birds, noisy birds which show fight and are left alone by the birds of prey. The Oriole is a brightly-coloured bird with yellow and black among its colours; but the Friar-bird is darker; and in order to share the protection of this noisy neighbour the Oriole has also become sombre. This is a case of mimicry.

But there is one nearer at hand. We can find at any time in the summer in our gardens the Drone-fly, which looks like a Honey-bee, but it is not. The Honey-bee can sting, and besides that, its insect enemies do not like its taste. But the Drone-fly cannot sting, and is good food for the birds which feed on insects. But these birds see them, and say to themselves: "We had better leave them alone; they are too much like those horrid bees."

The butterflies shown in our first illustration are closely related and distasteful to birds; the species shown in the other illustration, is unrelated and edible. It derives protection from its enemies by its similarity in precisely the same manner as the Drone-fly referred to above. There are innumerable similar examples which space does not permit us to include here.

*Photos]*                    *[H. Bastin.*
The butterflies shown in the top picture are distasteful to birds, and are mimicked by the species shown below, which by this means ward off their enemies.

# WHAT IS MEANT BY THE "MAN IN THE MOON"?

THE so-called "man in the moon" is the rude resemblance to a man's face presented by the moon's disc. It is, on the whole, wonderfully complete and well proportioned. The tip of his nose is always near the centre of the full moon and his left eye, we rather fancy, keeps winking at us. Other easily-recognizable features are his dark eyebrows and big, smudged mouth. When the moon is a thick crescent, we are able to make out, in a rough sort of way, his profile. All this, of course, is an optical effect only. The moon is a globe with a solid surface like the earth and the "man in the moon" is just mountain, crater, and valley forms, and nothing else ; it is simply the aspect of the lunar scenery as seen by we earth-dwellers at a distance of two hundred and forty thousand miles, where a whole hemisphere can be scanned at once. Rain, wind, and frost have carved the

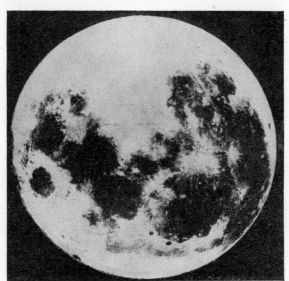

[From a photograph taken at the Yerkes Observatory, U.S.A.
The Moon is a globe with a solid surface like the earth, and the "man in the moon" is just mountain, crater, and valley forms, and nothing else.

rocks and crags of the English countryside into many equally strange figures and designs, and seen from afar, there would doubtless appear a "man (or some other living or inanimate shape) in the earth" as there is to us a "man in the moon." The moon's surface is incomparably more rugged and broken than anything on earth. In many places we should hardly be able to take a short evening ramble without being stopped by some enormous, gaping crevasse in the ground or by some unclimbable, precipitous peak or crag. And volcanic craters are so numerous that, with the best telescopes, over twenty-five thousand can be counted on the visible half of the moon's surface.

THE BLACK-AND-WHITE RUFFED LEMUR.

# WHY HAVE ANIMALS TAILS?

IF we see the skeleton of an animal and look along the backbone, at the end, we shall see a small or long series of bones making a tail which can bend easily. This gets smaller and smaller as it nears the end. The size of the tail depends upon the use that the animal can make of it. Some of the bears have very small tails; the hippo, too, has certainly not a tail to match his huge body.

[Carthew and Kinnaird, Ltd.

PARRY'S KANGAROO.

But there are creatures which have a tail twice or three times as long as their body. If we watch a cow on a summer's day when the flies are troubling her, we shall see one use of a tail; she has, indeed, a little tuft of hair at the end of it, which helps her to keep the flies away. There are monkeys which use their tails for climbing and for swinging on trees with their head downwards. Their tail has become specially fitted for this; that is what we mean by calling it *prehensile*. For some animals which live most of their lives in the water, the tail is useful as a rudder, and the mighty whale, which is not a fish but an animal, uses his tremendous tail as the means of moving through the water. The kangaroo in our picture on this page is shown using its tail as a rest and support.

# WHAT BIRD'S NEST SOMETIMES WEIGHS AS MUCH AS FIVE TONS?

THE natives of Australia knew about the nests which the Brush Turkey makes long before the white travellers found them in Queensland and New South Wales. This bird—the Wattled Talegallus, to give it its proper name—makes its nest in a retired glen on the slope of a hill. When the first traveller to find them came near, he noticed a part of the ground scratched clean ; and near to it a large mound of earth, chiefly consisting of black vegetable mould with decaying matter in it. Some of these mounds are surrounded by sticks ; these nests are at times as much as twelve feet across and thirty-four or thirty-six feet in circumference, and they may be two or three feet high. Some, indeed, are more like a pyramid in shape.

The male turkey scratches together with great patience the decaying matter ; he scratches it backward, as we might suppose, for it is much easier than kicking it forward. When it has become a heap, it is easy to see that, like a garden hotbed, it produces a strong heat within ; and when, in due time, the eggs are buried in this hot and steaming nest, they are eventually hatched, and the young turkeys come out of the big nest. More than one bird may use this nest ; and as many as thirty-six eggs may be buried in one heap.

[Fox Photos.

AN AUSTRALIAN BRUSH TURKEY ON ITS GIANT NEST.

# HOW IS CHEESE MADE?

CHEESE is made from milk, which is composed of curds and whey. The curd, or casein (" caseus " is the Latin word for cheese), is the solid part and contains much nitrogen, and in cheese-making the curds are thrown out of solution by the addition of rennet, which is obtained from the gastric juice extracted from the skin of the fourth stomach of the calf. This process of precipitation, or coagulation, is similar to that of the digestion which takes place in the human stomach. By keeping the liquid at the right tempera-ture, the cheese-maker is able to combine with the casein the greater part of the butter-fat present in the whey. For that matter, whenever milk turns sour and separates into a semi-solid and a liquid, we get the formation of a crude sort of cheese. There are many kinds of cheese—hard and soft—and some are named from the places where they are manufactured, such as the Roquefort shown in the picture above.

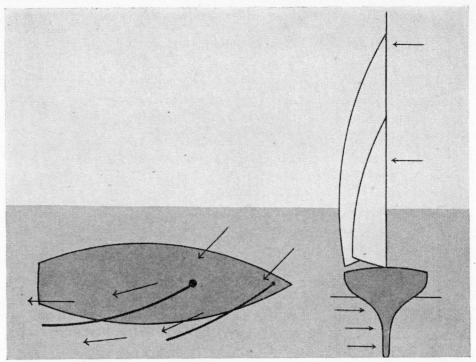

Fig. 1.    Sails deflect the wind astern causing force    Water pressure against the keel
tending to move the boat forward.    and wind pressure on the sails.

# HOW SHIPS SAIL AGAINST THE WIND?

THIS is accomplished by the setting of the sails and because of
the deep keel below the vessel in the water.   In Fig. 1 is a
plan view of a boat with a main sail and fore sail.   The wind
comes from the direction of the arrows on the right and is caught
and deflected by the sails in the direction of the arrows on the left.
Now if it were not for the deep keel the yacht would be blown
sideways, but the area of the keel in the water prevents this.   Try
pushing the flat side of a spade against the water and you will see
how this works.   In fact, with the wind deflected over the stern of
the boat and the keel preventing the boat blowing sideways, it must
go forwards.

The boat is still sailing at an angle of forty-five degrees to the
wind, however, so after sailing for some time in this direction it
must turn to the opposite " tack "—that is, so that the wind is

BULRUSH BOATS

The hull and sail of these boats, found on Lake Titicaca, the largest lake in South America, are made entirely from bulrushes. They can hold up to a dozen people. The pith is like cork, and makes them unsinkable.

THE DE HAVILLAND COMET—THE WORLD'S FIRST JET AIRLINER

blowing on the opposite side of the sail and still at forty-five degrees to the direction of the boat. In order to make progress towards a point directly to windward, the vessel must first sail with the wind on her starboard side, called the starboard tack, and then on the port tack —with the wind blowing on her port side. In Fig. 2 the vessel at A is on the port tack. After a while she turns so that the wind is on her starboard side and is thus on the starboard tack. At C the boat is turning from port to starboard tack, a manœuvre called " tacking" or "coming about" and the whole task of getting the boat from A to C, or as far as is necessary against the wind is called " beating to windward ".

A yachtsman who wishes to take up yacht racing needs plenty if experience of sailing a boat against the wind, as a yacht race usually follows a triangular course —to windward and back.

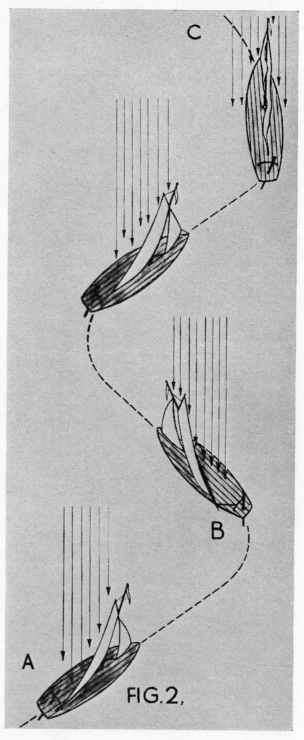

FIG. 2.

# HOW IS COAL FORMED?

TO understand how coal is formed, we must go back a very long way in the history of the earth—to an age long before man existed, and even probably when there were no animals. The only forms of life were vegetable ones, and coal is the fossilized remains of the forests which flourished in those far-off days. But these forests did not consist of the kinds of trees we find in our woods today ; they were more akin to our ferns and " mare's tails," though of gigantic size.

As time went on, the land densely covered with this vegetation was flooded with water and sank, and a layer of sand and mud was formed on the top of it, beneath which the vegetable matter would decay and fossilize. Then, as geologists have discovered, the whole mass was pushed up again above sea-level, and once more a new forest would grow, and once more the land would sink beneath the sea, and this would happen over and over again during enormously long periods of time.

This is the real explanation of why coal is always found in strata, or layers, known as " seams " ; it is as if a huge pile of sandwiches was being formed, the " meat " being the coal, and the place of the " bread " being occupied by the deposits of mud and sand. Gradually the great pressure and certain chemical changes converted the vegetable matter into coal ; one can get a good idea of what was happening by examining a block of peat, which is coal in the making.

It is, indeed, difficult to realise the vast number of years which have elapsed since the formation of coal began, especially when we are told that a layer one yard thick requires a thousand years in which to accumulate, and that certain coal fields in Wales are known to go down to a depth of over two miles. Coal is one of the most valuable substances we possess, and one wonders who it was who first gave it the apt nick-name of Black Diamonds. Interesting also it would, no doubt, be to know how long ago it was that some curious man, probably quite by accident, discovered that the strange black stones he found lying around would *burn* ! Coal not only keeps us warm, but with its aid we are able to obtain steam to drive our machinery and our trains and to generate electricity. In addition, we make from it innumerable useful substances such as dyes, perfumes, explosives and medicines.

A COAL CUTTER AT WORK.

# CAN YOU TAKE A PHOTO WITHOUT A LENS?

A PINHOLE PHOTOGRAPH.

**Y**ES, you can take a photograph without a lens, and without buying a camera from a shop, but the apparatus you can easily make and use for this purpose *is* really a camera, though a very simple one.

All you need is a small, well-made, light-proof box—such as a cigar box. Take out one of the sides, or a portion of one, and replace it with a thin sheet of metal, in the centre of which a very small opening, not larger than a pinhole, has been bored. If now you place a photographic plate against the side of the box facing the hole, you can obtain a good photograph which can be developed in the ordinary way. You should choose for your picture a stationary object, or a well-lit corner of the garden, because the rays of light entering the box through the tiny hole—which acts as a lens, are very feeble, and a long exposure (say of half an hour) is necessary. As focusing is impossible, one cannot determine definitely the amount of view included, and there will have to be a little guess-work. Our diagram illustrates a rough-and-ready method of getting over this difficulty. Make a central mark at the top back of the camera and mark out lines to each of the front corners Y Z. By looking along these lines, a rough idea of the view included can be gained.

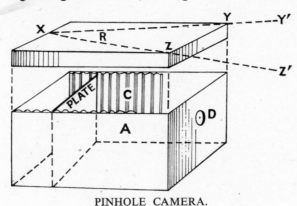

PINHOLE CAMERA.
A. Box. R. Close-fitting lid ; C. Corrugated paper to hold plate
D. Pinhole.

This "pinhole" camera of yours is a development of the old Camera Obscura, which was a small, darkened building, in the roof of which was fixed a box containing a convex lens and a sloping mirror which reflected a view of the country on to a table in the centre.

# HOW DO PLANTS FEED?

WHEN we view a large tree firmly rooted in the earth, we are apt to imagine that it grew from the soil. Actually, its several tons of solid wood came directly from the air in the form of carbon.

This carbon was captured by the leaves during sunlight, for the leaves are the mouths and stomachs of the plant.

If we burn a piece of dry wood, the mineral ash that is left (about

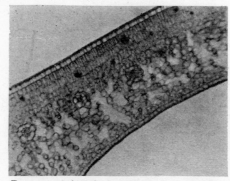

Transverse section of a Laurel leaf. By means of the green cells in the upper part of the leaf tissues. the carbonic acid gas of the atmosphere is converted into food materials.

two to seven per cent of its whole weight) represents practically all that came from the soil. The other materials have returned as gas and vapour to the air, from whence they came.

How, then, does the plant obtain this solid material by means of its leaves? The function of each leaf is to spread out its tissues into the air and absorb carbonic acid gas—the poisonous gas we exhale when breathing. Within the tissues of the green leaf this gas is broken up, and the carbon element it contains is retained and built into the plant structure to form starches, oils, and sugars. These energy-yielding substances are then utilised to convert the plant tissues into solid wood.

The plant, therefore, feeds from the air. Its water supply comes from the soil, together with its essential mineral ash in solution.

See also articles : *Why Leaves are Green*, page 206 and *How Plants Breathe*, page 240.

Photos]      [*John J. Ward.*
Transverse section of the twig of a bush, showing the first annual ring of wood growth formed from modification of vegetable cells shown in the centre.

A STREAMLINED STRATOCRUISER.

# WHY OUR CARS ARE STREAMLINED?

AIR has weight, although we do not notice it unless the wind is blowing, because we are so accustomed to it in our life. When a motor car or train travels forward, it has to push aside the air, and, since the air has weight, this uses up energy. The amount of energy required to push aside the air depends upon the size and speed of the surface which is doing this pushing. The two are related and engineers say that the " resistance " of the air increases as the square of the speed. In other words the amount of pushing required increases very greatly in proportion to the speed.

Streamlining is the method by which the " resistance " of the air is reduced, and hence the amount of energy required to overcome it. This is first accomplished by making the surface pushing into the air as small as possible. A piece of card pushed edgeways cuts the air more easily than when it is pushed with the full face to the front. The frontal surface of a car or a train is much smaller than its longitudinal surface. But it has been found that there is more in streamlining than this. Not only the weight of the air, but also eddies and currents set up by the forward movement hold back a car. Therefore, designers make the lines of the vehicle " clean " so that the air can sweep past without setting up eddies or creating

# WHY OUR CARS ARE STREAMLINED?

a vacuum at the back. A streamlined object will set up less resistance than an oddly-shaped one which is actually smaller, and this explains why modern aeroplanes have " spats " on their wheels.

[*Mirrorpic.*

AIR RESISTANCE IS AN IMPORTANT FACTOR IN MOTOR RACING.

# CAN ANIMALS TALK?

THE answer must be—some can. It is one of the things which mark animals off one from another, that some do not talk and others do. What we call the lower animals do not talk. It has been said that of all vertebrate animals, that is animals with a spinal column, the amphibians were the first to have a voice. When we hear a frog croaking in the spring-time, we know that this is the oldest of voices. The sound of the voice is due to the fact that the air from the lungs passes over the cords stretched in the larynx and makes a vibration. And this kind of musical instrument has been used for various purposes. At first it was the call of the male to the female; then it was the way in which the mother called to her young, or the young to their mother; then it was used to give warning when danger was near, or to carry news. Monkeys seem able to tell each other a good deal, but it is only when we come to man that we find these vibrations made by the air passing through the larynx became the means of expressing thought and purpose. But when the lion roars after its prey, or the great speaker talks in Parliament, they both use the same musical instrument, and both are animals. But what a difference there is !

By courtesy of]                                                    [Carl Hagenbeck.
### ABYSSINIAN OR SACRED BABOONS.
Most monkeys seem able to tell each other a great deal.

[B.O.A.C

A BABY CHIMPANZEE, FLOWN TO ENGLAND FROM WEST AFRICA.

# TELL ME, PLEASE?

1. Which comes first in a thunderstorm, the thunder or the lightning?
2. What is the origin of the name dragoon?
3. When is Candlemas?
4. What is another name for a young eagle?
5. What is the origin of the word " terminus "?
6. What is a mandarin?
7. What is the origin of the military salute?
8. How did Covent Garden get its name?
9. What do we mean by " The Black Maria "?
10. For what do we use rennet?
11. What is : (*a*) a barnevelder, (*b*) a barnstormer?
12. What is amber?
13. What day is the longest in the year?
14. What day is the shortest in the year?

*For answers to these questions, see p.* 122.

# ANSWERS TO QUESTIONS on page 121

1. The lightning.
2. It originated from the fact that in the olden days the short muskets the regiment carried were called " dragons."
3. February 2nd.
4. Aiglet.
5. From the Roman God of Boundaries, who was called Terminus.
6. A Chinese official of high rank.
7. To show that no weapon was concealed in the hand.
8. It was once the garden of the Convent of Westminster.
9. A police van for the conveyance of accused persons.
10. In order to curdle milk, especially when making junket.
11. (a) A breed of poultry, (b) a strolling player.
12. Translucent oxidised resin, found chiefly on the shores of the Baltic.
13. June 21st.
14. December 21st.

[*Keystone.*

PACKING TINNED PEAS.

[Batchelor's Peas, Ltd.

STERILIZING PEAS IN AUTOMATIC COOKERS.

# HOW ARE PEAS CANNED?

THE peas in the pod brought in from the fields are shelled by feeding them into a machine called a "podder". After being blanched in boiling water, the peas are mechanically filled at the correct weight and temperature at a speed of about 120 cans per minute. The weight is carefully checked, and a covering liquid is added so that heat applied in the sterilizing process is rapidly conveyed through the can.

The cans then pass through a heating tunnel called an exhaust box and are heated to a temperature of more than 160° Fahrenheit before being sealed in order to create a vacuum. A machine called a double seamer adds the lids of the cans, and they are then sterilized in automatic cookers.

During the process of sterilization, the peas are fully cooked and only require reheating before being served. The cans are then cooled to a temperature of about 100° F., and fed on to the runway of a labelling machine. Finally, they are packed into fibre-board or corrugated board cartoons, holding one or more dozen cans.

[*U.S. Information Service.*

### LARGEST TELESCOPE IN THE WORLD.

Situated on Mount Palomar, in California, this giant telescope has a 200-inch mirror and rises 138 feet from the ground.  It has revolutionised astronomical research, and has already proved that the earth is at least 1.000,000,000 years old.

# HOW FAR AWAY ARE THE STARS?

EVERY star in the sky is a great, brilliant sun like ours whose splendour is dimmed by distance only to a mere pin-point of light. This fact only should impress us as to how vast this distance must be. The lovely globular cluster of stars in the constellation called Hercules, sends out two and a half million times as much light as the sun, yet very keen eyes are needed to see it at all without magnifying glasses. The nearest star to the earth (apart from the

[*Mount Wilson Observatory.*

STAR CLOUDS IN SAGITTARIUS.

sun) is about twenty-five millions of millions of miles away. Even light, travelling at the amazing speed of one hundred and eighty-six thousand miles a second, requires roughly four years and three months to cover such a distance. We therefore see the very nearest of stars not as it is to-day, *but as it was four and a quarter years ago.* Similarly, when we look at the most distant star in our own galaxy, we are peering back two hundred and fifty thousand years into the past. And there are nebulae (see " What is a Nebula " ? page 52) six hundred times farther off still.

# TELL ME WHY?

Our own Solar System is part of the Milky Way. This consists of a belt of stars covering the whole of the heavens visible to us. It is believed that the Milky Way forms a universe, with a rotation different to that of the other universes we can just see with the aid of powerful telescopes. As we cannot even see the individual stars in nebulae, we have no idea just how far away from us they are.

See also our article: *How many Stars are there*? page 223, which shows that the earth ranks as little more than a speck of dust.

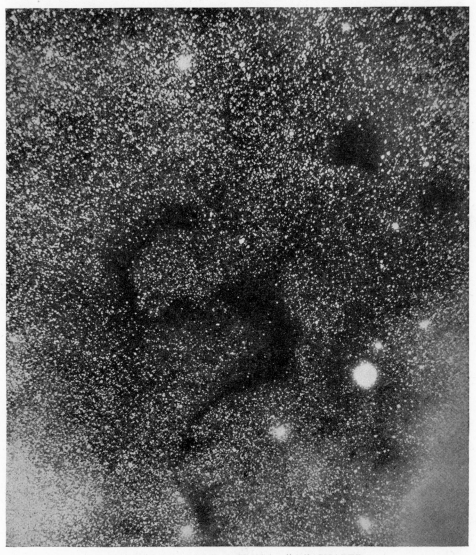

OPHIUCHUS DARK NEBULA—"S" SHAPED.

[E. N. A.

AFTER A VAIN ATTEMPT TO EXTRACT THE YOKE OF AN OSTRICH EGG,
THIS MONGOOSE TURNS ITS ATTENTION TO A HEN'S EGG.

# WHAT IS A MONGOOSE?

WE call it *mongoose* to-day, but the ancient Egyptians, who thought it a sacred animal, called it the ichneumon. If we look for it in the old pictures of Egypt, we must think of a creature like a long weasel ; its hair looks speckled ; its nose is short and the ears small ; the legs are short, and the feet have five toes ; and all mongooses have long, straight claws.

The mongoose is still found in Africa, but it is best known in India. There it is found in every part, from north to south ; it can be found in hedgerows, on banks of streams and in groves of trees, but not in the dense forests. Its chief value to human beings is due to its taste in food. It has, indeed, a very big appetite, and it likes best rats and mice and lizards, eggs and insects, but especially snakes. One traveller tells how he found inside one mongoose " a quail, a small wasps' nest, a lizard, a number of insects and part of a custard-apple."

It is a very fierce little creature. It is always ready to fight a snake. When the snake darts at it, it pounces upon its head and bites it at the back of the neck, usually severing the spine. Because it is so wonderfully quick, it usually escapes from the bite of a snake. But fierce as it is to the snakes, it is easily tamed and makes an affectionate pet.

# HOW WE WEIGH THE EARTH?

ISAAC NEWTON took the first step towards weighing the earth when he watched an apple falling, and decided that both the falling of the apple and the moon's motion in the sky must be governed by the same force—the earth's gravitation. He found that the gravitational force between two bodies was always proportional to their masses ; and that it was also inversely proportional to the square of the distance between them. That means that if we double the mass of one of the bodies, we will double the gravitational force ; and that if we halve the distance, we shall increase the force four-fold. Now we know what the pull of the earth is at its surface and how far

away the centre of the earth is. Therefore we can calculate the mass of the earth, if we can only measure the gravitational pull between two bodies, the masses and positions of which we know in advance. This involves a laboratory experiment of great accuracy. A pair of gold balls are hung from a light cross-bar, hung from a very fine quartz fibre. The extent to which the fibre is twisted when two heavier lead balls are brought close to the gold provides a measure of the gravitational force between them.

It is estimated the world weighs in the neighbourhood of 6,000,000,000,000,000,000 tons. The picture shows the apparatus used to form this estimate. It consists merely of two heavy bronze weights, two little bronze marbles, a couple of strands of wire, a mirror, a concrete block and a telescope.

[Gibson & Sons.

A GUILLEMOT, RAZOR BILLS AND A SHAG.

# TELL ME, PLEASE?

1. What do we mean by a ruminant?

2. What do we call a camel with one hump only?

3. How did the secretary bird get its name?

4. What are amphibians?

5. What is a dingo?

6. What is pewter?

7. How does a dog perspire?

8. How did dandelions get their name?

9. What was the Renaissance?

10. Who was St. Swithin?

11. What is a pangolin?

12. Which cathedral in England has the highest spire?

*For answers to these questions, see page* 130.

# ANSWERS TO QUESTIONS on page 129

1. An animal that chews its cud.

2. A dromedary.

3. Because of the quill-like feathers on both sides of the head.

4. Animals that can live either on land or in water.

5. A wild, or half-domesticated, dog of Australia.

6. A silvery-grey alloy of tin and lead.

7. Through its tongue.

8. From the French " dent de lion," referring to the toothed edges of the leaves.

9. The revival of learning and art which spread through Europe during the 14th 15th, and 16th centuries.

10. Bishop of Winchester in 852.

11. A species of scaly ant-eater that rolls itself up into a ball for protection, in the same way as a hedgehog.

12. Salisbury, 404 feet high.

[*Sport & General.*

A BEAVER HOUSE OR "LODGE", WITH A BEAVER AT WORK
ON THE ROOF.

BEAVERS AT WORK.

# HOW A BEAVER BUILDS HIS DAM?

THERE was a time when in Europe many beavers could be found ; in our own country the names of places like Beverley tell of days in which these clever and sociable animals had their colonies here. Now it is in the New World that we must look if we want to see their homes. They are at home in the water, being most clever swimmers and divers ; they are among the creatures who are wide awake at night when we are asleep ; and, though they eat the roots of water-lilies and such things for a treat, their chief diet is the bark and the twigs of trees. In America they can still be found in companies. In order to live in comfort, they must have a large lake or pond with water deep enough for them to swim when the ice covers the surface. They choose a small stream with trees on the banks. Then they set to work to fell the trees. They have sharp teeth with which they gnaw through the stems at a little distance above the ground. When the trees fall, the beavers take

131

away all the branches, and cut the trunk of the tree into lengths of five or six feet. The bark of the trees gives them their dinner ; and the bare pieces of timber are rolled by them into the stream and used to form a dam, which is the name given to a bank or other barrier raised to keep back water. Sometimes in a stream there will be many such pools or lakes made by these clever creatures. The dam may be one hundred and fifty yards long. It is smeared with mud, like plaster, so that the water does not get through it. In the summer the beavers go up and down the stream but in winter they come back to their home behind the dam.

It is a wonderful fact that in felling a tree the beavers nearly always get it to fall in the right direction—towards the water, to save the labour of rolling it. Is not it wonderful, too, that the other members of the colony are rarely hurt or killed by the falling trees ?

## WHAT IS MANNA ?

IF you have noticed the blobs of gum which appear on the trunk of a plum tree when its bark has been damaged, you will understand the source of manna. It is a sweetish, whitey-brown substance which oozes through slits cut in the bark of tamarisk trees growing in Sicily and other parts of southern Europe. Formerly it was much used as a laxative medicine for children, and its sugary flavour must have been a pleasant change from the nasty senna tea with which the youngsters of our grandfathers' day were often dosed.

We read in the book of Exodus (Chapter XVI) that the Israelites, during their wanderings in the wilderness, were fed on manna, but probably this was a kind of lichen found growing on rocks, which is detached by the wind and carried long distances.

## WHAT ARE FRECKLES ?

IF you saw four people of different nationalities, you would notice that their skins were of different colours—a Norwegian, " fair " ; an Italian, " olive " ; a Chinese, " yellow " ; and a Negro, " black." All skins are coloured and the colour depends on the deposit in the deeper layers of microscopical dark granules called " pigment."

If a person has "pigment" deposited in small patches, instead of evenly you get the appearance called " freckles." They occur mostly in " fair " or " red-skinned " people.

A Praying Mantis (natural size) posing as a flower in order to attract its prey.

# WHAT IS A PRAYING MANTIS?

WE have no reason to think that insects pray, but one certainly looks as if it does. With its head bowed and its arms folded, the *mantis* has the look of an insect worshipping. But we should be wrong if we thought it a quiet and kind insect at prayer. We do not say that it is pretending, because it cannot know what its bowed head means to us. As a matter of fact, it is thinking when it looks most quiet of the food that it needs. It moves only slowly, and is not made for flight, so that it must use all its arts to get its food. It takes the colour of its surroundings, green, chiefly, or brown. It is rather a greedy insect and not at all merciful in its ways. It seizes its food with its shears, and bites its victims bit by bit. Sir J. A. Thomson says that, when it is feeding, it is like a schoolboy eating an apple, and between bites stopping to watch it getting less and less. It is also very wasteful and thinks nothing of leaving half its victim uneaten and starting on another. Some think that when it has started killing, it likes it so much that it wants to go on, and does not finish one victim before attacking another.

[A. W. Kerr, L.E.A.

A STRIKING PICTURE OF BEACHY HEAD LIGHTHOUSE,
TAKEN DURING A GALE.

WAVES BREAKING ON THE SHORE.

# WHAT MAKES A WAVE BREAK?

A WAVE breaks because it has no room to bounce. When a wave advances to the beach, the water itself is not moving inwards. If it were, the beach would soon be flooded out. All the water is doing is to move up and down, the movement being handed on from one " piece " of water to the next, until the beach is reached. But some distance before reaching the beach the water has not enough room to move freely up and down. So it breaks instead into the confused sort of motion that we call breaking.

Big waves naturally represent a proportionately bigger up and down movement and so they break farther out at sea. When the wind blows the tops off big waves and we see the " White horses " out at sea, we know it's rough ; but this is quite a different kind of wave break from that encountered on the seashore.

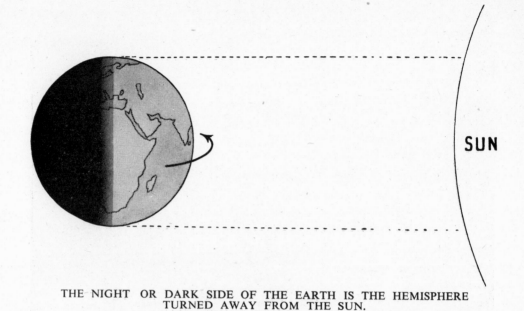

SUN

THE NIGHT OR DARK SIDE OF THE EARTH IS THE HEMISPHERE
TURNED AWAY FROM THE SUN.

# WHY IS IT DARK AT NIGHT?

THE earth we live on is a rotating globe lit up entirely by the rays from another and far greater self-luminous globe which we call the sun. It is dark at night, therefore, simply because only one half of the earth's surface can be illuminated at once, and at night we are on the unilluminated side or half. The night, or dark side, of the earth is the hemisphere turned away from the sun, and when on it the solar rays cannot get at us—we are, so to speak, round the corner and out of their way. Our world is like a man turning round and round in front of a fire; first one side (half) of him is exposed to its light and heat and then the other. The earth's turning, however, is nothing like so simple as this. On account of its varied and peculiar motions, the exposed (day) and unexposed (night) sides (halves) are never exactly the same for two days in succession. They are always changing throughout the twelve months. The hemisphere that is dark today will not in its entirety be the dark hemisphere again till this time next year. And neither, of course, will the lighted hemisphere. This is just another way of saying that the lengths of the days and nights at any one place are constantly changing. We all know that it gets dark a minute or two sooner or later tomorrow than today.

136

# WHY SOAP MAKES US CLEAN?

SOAPS consist chiefly of fatty oils with an alkali and originally, it was thought that they made our hands clean because of the alkali. Now it is realised that there is much too little alkali present for this, and that washing is a physical, rather than a chemical, action. The soap bubbles do not dissolve the dirt, but " absorb " or float it in colloidal solution, and the dirt is thus prevented from being re-deposited upon your hands. This is shown by the great difficulty of filtering out the dirt in soapy water. Soap also acts by lubricating the dirt and making its removal by rubbing very much easier.

The effectiveness of soap depends partly upon the concentration, and too much soap is sometimes as bad as too little. In the case of some soaps, chemicals are added for extra cleansing, but these are not usually good for the hands. Whale oil, coconut oil, palm oil and olive oil are all used in the manufacture of soap.

[Fox Photos.

HAVING A GOOD WASH.

137

WHAT AN UGLY FELLOW !

The Proboscis Monkey is so-called because of its long, flexible nose.

# HOW A FRONT-DOOR LOCK WORKS?

THESE two views (figs. 1 and 2) show a latch lock for front-doors. A barrel or cylinder A (fig. 1) can rotate in the lock case B and carries the lever C which withdraws the bolt D to open the lock.

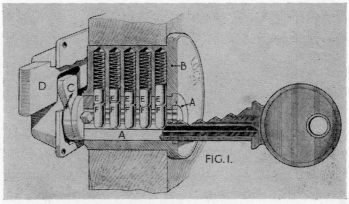

FIG. I.

The key is about to be inserted in the lock. Note the position of the spring-pressed plungers E and F.

Sets of spring-pressed plungers E and F lock the cylinder to the lock case when in the position shown in fig. 1. They are of different heights. The key has inclines of different heights on its edge, and when pushed into the cylinder, these inclines on the key raise the plungers till, as shown in fig. 2, they are all in line along the edge of the cylinder A and the edge of the lock case B so that the cylinder can be turned by the key, turning with it the lever C (in the direction of the arrow), and pushing back the door bolt D. A spring behind bolt D returns it to the locked position when pressure on key is released ; and when key is withdrawn, the plungers fall down again and lock all together.

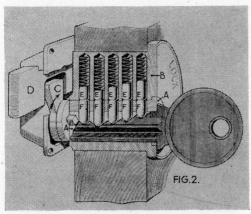

FIG. 2.

Here the key is fully inserted. Note the " wiggley-waggley" shape of the key and the position of the various spring-pressed plungers E and F.

The keyhole itself has a "wiggley-waggley" shape and the key a shape to fit. Another shaped key could not be inserted. Different locks have different shapes.

All the locks have plungers of different heights, and the incline on the keys must correspond for each lock and each key. Millions of combinations are available, so the chances of one key fitting another lock are far more than a million to one.

Mondiale] [James Hornell.

This boy in the Canary Islands is carrying bags of female cochineal insects, to be hung upon cactus plant leaves, upon which they feed.

# WHAT IS COCHINEAL?

WE have all seen things, sweets perhaps, dyed scarlet ; and we have learned that the dye used is called " cochineal," which is a word taken from the Latin for scarlet. But we may not have known that this beautiful colour is made from certain dead insects. The insect belongs to the general class of scale-insects ; the male has only one pair of wings, the female has none ; and in many parts of the world they are considered only a nuisance and an enemy to be fought. In Mexico and Central America there are some of these half-winged creatures which have proved very valuable. The mother is brown in colour. She lays a thousand eggs, and the insects swarm everywhere. When they are large enough, they are threaded together, put in bags, and then thrown into boiling water. Then they are dried, and from these dead insects the scarlet dye is made. It is said that seventy thousand of them, all female, go to one pound of cochineal.

It should be mentioned that this insect feeds on the cactus.

140

# IS THERE A BIRD WITHOUT WINGS?

WHEN we see living creatures, it is never safe to trust first impressions. The penguin, for example, can swim, and can walk, but cannot fly ; nevertheless it is a bird ; it has wings which do not enable it to fly. There are other birds which cannot be said to be without wings exactly, but the wings are not developed. Of these *Running Birds* there are five kinds. The African ostrich ; the American ostrich ; the emu ; the cassowary, and the kiwi. The kiwi, which is a New Zealand bird, has its name because of its cry. It is more properly called *apteryx*, which means *without wings ;* and such it is. It is a bird which can move quickly and hide itself among the ferns. Today we hear that it is a bird which may die out and become extinct. The kiwi is about the size of an ordinary hen, but it lays an enormous egg. It comes out for its food in the night, and it has a long beak which enables it to strike its victim. Why is it unable to fly ? Some think that it is a very old kind of creature, surviving from the most ancient times before birds flew and it has always been without the use of wings.

*By courtesy of]* [*The High Commissioner for New Zealand.*
THE KIWI, OR APTERYX, NEW ZEALAND'S WINGLESS BIRD.

# WHY DOES THE SUN RISE AND SET?

THE sun rises and sets for the same reason that it is dark at night, namely, because we live on the surface of a rotating ball or globe called the earth. The rotation of the earth carries us now into the light of day and now into the shades of night. We are now on the side or hemisphere facing the sun and now we are on the hemisphere turned away and hidden from it. The moment the sun is above our horizon, we are on the hemisphere facing the sun and daylight begins. (Which, incidentally, is always earlier than we think, for when we see the sun rising, it actually rose above the the horizon eight minutes ago, because its beams take over eight minutes to reach our eyes.) The instant the sun disappears below our horizon, we are on the hemisphere turned away from the sun and night begins. The sun has been below our horizon (and night has already begun) eight minutes as we see it setting. The whirling earth carrying us from the dark to the lighted side causes the sun to rise. Conversely, carrying us from the lighted side into the dark side causes the sun to set. At every single moment of the twenty-four hours, it is noon somewhere, midnight somewhere, sunrise somewhere, and sunset somewhere.

# WHAT FISH SHOOTS ITS PREY?

WHEN by the riverside, we sometimes see fishes shooting their noses out of the water to reach flies hovering near the surface. Probably, as often as not, the fly is brought down by merely being wetted with the water thrown up by the fish, as most flying insects have a tendency suddenly to drop when touched.

It is the Archer-fish (*Toxotes jaculator*), which inhabits the rivers of the East Indies, Australia, and New Zealand, that has made the most of that discovery. Instead of jerking itself out of the water, it acquired the art of lying low with a mouthful of water in readiness to shoot, as a single globule, like a bullet, at the unwary fly.

From quite simple beginnings, its skill as a marksman steadily evolved. Now the fish favours the shallows of rivers with over-hanging foliage on which flies alight. It then takes sight of a resting fly and makes a perfect aim, knocking it off and capturing it.

It is said the fish can bring down flies at a distance of six feet.

# WHY DOES SMOKE RISING STRAIGHT UP INDICATE FINE WEATHER ?

MANY of the countryman's weather signs have a solid foundation. Smoke rising straight up, for example, is often an indication that the observer is near the middle of an anticyclone. That is, a region of piled-up air, which is quiet in the middle, with winds circulating round it outside. An anticyclone is often very stable and, therefore, corresponds with settled weather. In summer, this means a fine, hot spell ; in winter, an anticyclone may produce great cold and, perhaps, fog. But if by fine weather we mean absence of rain, then the omen generally works.

[*Keytsone.*

SMOKE RISING STRAIGHT UP IS INVARIABLY ACCEPTED BY COUNTRY MEN AS AN INDICATION OF FINE WEATHER.

# WHY IS RAIN-WATER SOFT?

HARD water is " hard " because it has dissolved a certain proportion of mineral salts between the time when it fell from
the sky as rain and the time it reaches our houses. The hardness, in
fact, comes from the ground, chalky water being notoriously hard.
Now rain-water is really distilled water, which, as we know, is
specially pure. It has been evaporated from the surface of seas,
lakes and rivers. When it is evaporated, it takes no mineral salts
with it, so that unless it has been polluted by falling through a
town fog, it is very nearly pure. It has had no chance to become
" hard."

# WHY HAVE SOME BIRDS BRIGHT PLUMAGE?

A BIRD may be handsomely adorned with feathers of many
colours, while its neighbour, of a different family, may be
gorgeously attired in the most brilliant splendour, with merely a
few of the colours of the other bird.

Everything depends on what we mean by colour, whether
produced by pigments, structural details, or a combination of both.

Where the colouring is due to chemical pigments, a showy effect
may be produced, but one that lacks in iridescence and brilliancy.
When, however, the structural or physical comes into play, then
brilliancy and rainbow colours commence to appear.

Combined with a pigment base, these rainbow-like colours give
the glossy, metallic sheen to the peacock's train, the cock birds of
paradise their bright patches, and the glistening ornamentations of
the cock humming birds.

It is the minute structure of the feathers that produces the
flashing and sheening colours. The fine strands and layers of the
barbs in the vane of the feather break up the rays of white light and
show colour effects—just as do glass prisms.

Since the microscopic layers and ridges are arranged on various
planes, they produce different colour displays according to their
particular interference of the light rays. The best effects are attained
when this breaking up of the light rays is assisted by a favourable
pigmentary ground.

# HOW DO BATS "SEE"?

OF all living creatures, probably the bat is the one most familiar to all the inhabitants of the world. It is found almost everywhere. If a whale is a mammal which swims, a bat is a mammal which flies, and all its make-up is designed for that purpose. It moves about chiefly by night; and its eyes are very small; we say that a man is as "blind as a bat," but it is not true that the bat is blind. Bats do not need very large eyes, because they are able to avoid objects by their sense of touch, which, it seems is unusually strong.

Some creatures do not need quick eyes, because they have a strong sense of smell. But bats trust to their sense of touch, which is found in the wing membranes and also in their ears, which have something within them like an inner ear. This is a sharply-pointed membrane, sometimes referred to as the second ear, but properly known as the tragus. It is noted that

[*Ray Palmer.*

A BARBASTELLE BAT IN FLIGHT.

the bats which live on fruits, and do not need the same quickness of touch, have not got this inner ear. There are, of course, many different kinds of bats. Most of them have mouse-like heads, adorned by exceedingly large ears. Their extraordinarily large wings are umbrella-like in construction and the feet are furnished with hook-like claws, by means of which they hang when at rest.

A very long time ago, in 1793, some bats were blinded and put in a room across which silken threads were drawn; they had just space to get through them with their wings spread out; they did this, blind as they were supposed to be, without difficulty; indeed, they moved about as freely, avoiding the walls and ceiling, as if they had their eyesight. This does not mean that bats are blind, but that they have other means, as well as their eyes, of knowing where they are.

[*Topical Press.*

The American Aloe, which only flowers once in every hundred years, in flower near Dartmouth, Devon. The bloom rises to a height of thirty feet.

The arid and furrowed surface of Death Valley, California. One of the most remarkable but forbidding regions in the world.

# HOW OLD IS THE EARTH?

MINERALS like radium are called radioactive because they give off rays and change of their own accord with the mere passage of time, into totally different substances. The rate at which this change takes place has been measured with extreme precision, and moreover, it appears to be absolutely unalterable. The most violent changes of temperature or other conditions fail to affect it —do not speed it up or slow it down in the least degree. As these radioactive substances are found in the rocks of all countries, they have proved to be the master-key to the time-secrets of old Mother Earth. They tell us that the very oldest rocks solidified approximately fourteen hundred million years ago. And before a hard crust had formed on her outside, Mother Earth is judged to have existed in the vaporous and liquid state for millions, and probably for some hundreds of millions of years. Astronomical evidence also tends to show that the solar system, of which the earth is a planetary member, must be a very few thousands of millions of years old.

As a round number estimate, the age of the earth is invariably given as two thousand million years.

# WHERE COFFEE COMES FROM ?

OUR coffee supplies come largely from the tropics of the New World, Brazil producing more than two-thirds of the world's supply. That is the more remarkable since the coffee shrub is a native of the fertile mountains at the south-west of Abyssinia. Indeed, the word coffee is said to be derived from Caffa, the name of one of the provinces of that country.

The custom of drinking coffee probably originated with the Abyssinians, but, early in the fifteenth century, it was introduced into Arabia, where it was more largely used, and, later, that country supplied the world.

[Dorien Leigh, Ltd.

A WOMAN COFFEE PICKER IN KENYA.

In 1718, from a coffee plant cultivated in the botanical gardens at Amsterdam, some seeds were conveyed to Surinam, in Dutch Guiana, and, so far as is known, that was the origin of all the vast coffee plantations of the New World.

Later, the West Indies and Java had supplanted Arabia in producing the world's supplies, and then came Brazil with overwhelming quantities. To-day coffee is Brazil's main industry, upwards of 2,000,000,000 lbs. being exported annually.

While Turkey and Arabia produce the best grades of coffee, the products of the Central American Republic of Costa Rica, together with those of the Kenya Colony of East Africa, satisfy largely British taste.

India is the principal coffee-growing region in the British Commonwealth and exports largely to England, chiefly from Mysore.

The coffee shrub (*Coffea arabica*) may grow from fifteen to twenty feet in height, but, under cultivation, is usually kept to about twelve feet in order to facilitate the gathering of its berries. It bears clusters of sweet-scented, white flowers, which are succeeded by red, fleshy berries, each containing two seeds—coffee beans.

When the beans are freed from their fruity covering and outer skin, they are washed and dried. Afterwards they undergo the process of roasting.

## WHERE WATER IS PRECIOUS.
A water-seller in the land of the Pyramids.  The water is carried in the skin on the man's back.

TREACHEROUS, BOGGY LAND IN IRELAND.                    [*Topical Press.*

# HOW A BOG IS FORMED?

A BOG, or peat-moss as it is sometimes called, is usually a lake or other standing body of water that is in process of being converted into firm ground by the steady growth of vegetation. The formation of a bog from a lake can be seen actually going on in many parts of the world. Mossy little plants can be seen growing into the water right round the circumference of many a moorland pool or mere. And the nearby soil is found, upon examination, to be made of a peculiar black or brown spongy substance called peat, which consists entirely of the dead and decaying roots and fibres of these very same mossy plants matted together. At the bottom of a bog and underlying the peat, geologists sometimes find a layer of clay containing fresh-water shells and perhaps flint implements, a wooden canoe and other relics of prehistoric man. This clay, of course, was the bottom of the ancient and now filled-up lake. The slopes which surround the flat surface of the boggy area were the banks of the original lake. Once a lake, afterwards a bog or mire, now firm, heather clad moor. That seems to be the history of a boggy district. Where the lake and bog has already been turned into dry, hard turf, it is usually pleasantly springy and yielding to the tread, and a walking stick may be thrust down a foot or more deep with ease. Ireland has over three million acres of bogland,

and it is significant that Ireland is as much noted for its loughs (lakes) as its bogs.

[*Will F. Taylor.*

CUTTING PEAT IN THE BOG OF ALLEN, IRELAND.

151

# HOW WE MEASURE THE EARTH'S CIRCUMFERENCE?

BOATS appear over the horizon. So do stars when they rise. Stars rise and set because the earth is curved, and the measurement of the height of the same star above the horizon in different latitudes tells us the circumference of the earth. If you think of the earth as a round ball, you will have no difficulty in realizing that the Pole Star is always on the horizon for an observer at the equator. Now suppose that our observer moves due north for a certain number of miles and takes a surveyor with him to measure the distance exactly. At the end of his journey he will find that the Pole Star has risen so many degrees in the sky. That means that the observer's latitude is now so many degrees north, for it is a matter of simple geometry to show that the angle through which the Pole Star has risen is equal to the angle through which the observer has moved as viewed from the centre of the earth. He will find that a degree of latitude is equal to between six and seven miles. If the earth were strictly round, this figure would always remain the same, however far he moved north. Actually it decreases slightly in higher latitudes, the decrease being a measure of the extent to which the earth is flattened at the poles. The earth's polar diameter works out at seven thousand nine hundred miles, and its equatorial diameter at seven thousand nine hundred and twenty-seven miles.

# HOW A PULLEY WORKS?

A PULLEY consists of a grooved wheel which can carry a rope revolving inside a frame and is designed either for transmitting power or for making the lifting of heavy weights easier. When weights are to be lifted, two sets of pulleys, one fixed and the other movable, usually with a hook, are used. Each set of pulleys contains two, three, or more wheels and the rope is carried continuously between them, one end being fixed. It will be seen that the loose end of rope travels much farther than the pulley carrying the hook. If there are three wheels to each pulley, the rope will travel six times as far as the pulley, and thus anyone hauling on the rope will be able to lift a weight which normally would be beyond him.

*[Sport & General.*

BIG GAME OF THE OCEAN.

Hauling aboard a huge tunny, weighing over 600 lbs. These great fish are caught by rod and line, and furnish wonderful sport. Without a pulley they would be very difficult to haul on board.

153

WEIGHING SCRAP METAL FOR FOUNDRY CASTING.

The ingots into which they are cast are then sold again to the engineers and manufacturers.

# WHAT HAPPENS TO SCRAP METAL?

**B**ECAUSE metal is almost indestructible, and things made of metal wear out and become disused, there is always a lot of scrap metal which is collected and sold to the scrap metal merchants who deal with all metals. These include ferrous metals, i.e. those made of iron, such as wrought iron, cast iron, steel, etc., and non-ferrous metals such as copper, tin, lead, etc., and alloys such as pewter (made of tin and antimony), brass (made of copper-zinc and a small amount of tin) and the bronzes, which are alloys of copper and tin. Also, in the manufacturing and engineering trades " swarf " is produced. It is the cuttings, filings, etc., of the metals being machined, and will contain many metals, ferrous and non-ferrous.

First, all metals are sorted. The fine shavings and cuttings are passed through a magnetic separator in which electric magnets attract all the iron or ferrous metals and allow the non-ferrous metals to pass. The latter are melted down to make the various alloys and the iron goes to the blast furnace to make wrought and cast iron or steel. Larger pieces are sorted on travelling platforms which bring the pieces before the sorters, who pass them to other travelling platforms where each sort is collected. When all are sorted out, they are sold by weight to the founders, who melt them and cast them into ingots to be sold again.

A "FLYING FISH".

# CAN FISH FLY?

WHEN on a cruise in tropical and sub-tropical seas, shoals of flying fishes may not infrequently be seen flashing their iridescent colours in the sunlight as they rise above the waves.

These fishes, of herring-like form, are about twelve inches in length, and have enormously-developed pectoral, or breast fins, which constitute their so-called wings and extend almost to the tail.

There are numerous species, all of surface-swimming habits, and probably they fly to escape from the attacks of predatory fishes. Their appearance before an approaching steamer merely implies alarm at being disturbed. Having once witnessed a shoal making their beautiful flight, skimming the tops of the on-coming waves, and covering spans of from three hundred to five hundred feet, at a speed from ten to twenty yards per second, one might feel justified in stating that fishes can fly. On that point, however, there is much controversy amongst naturalists. The difficulty is to decide whether the fins are flapped in the air to sustain flight, like the wings of a bird, or are merely used as planes to support the fish whilst gliding over the air waves.

What appears certain is that the fish gets its initial impetus from the water with powerful strokes of the tail, and that when it sinks to the surface and touches the water with its tail, it can again rise, but there is no definite proof of power gained in the air.

Some observers maintain that the fishes while in the air vibrate their fins at an extremely rapid pace, invisible to the eye.

There are also flying gurnards, and a Congo fresh-water fish, that use their fins as wings.

# WHICH IS THE BIGGEST SPIDER?

THE largest British Garden, or Orb-weaving, Spider has a rotund body about three-quarters of an inch long, with legs extending to a similar length.

There are also House Spiders of the genus *Tegenaria* with a body about the same length as that of the largest web-weavers of our gardens, but with legs more than twice the length of their bodies.

Now imagine a spider with a body a good three inches long, with powerful, hairy legs spanning fully nine inches. That would, indeed, seem a monster !

Such is the size of some of the large Avicularid, or Bird-eating Spiders of the tropics, often wrongly called Tarantulas—a much smaller species.

These large spiders live amongst the branches of trees, and do not spin a snare. They hunt their prey of small birds, mice, and lizards, as well as grasshoppers, locusts and other insects.

They inhabit most tropical countries, and, not infrequently, they are brought to England with bananas. They live in captivity for several years if well fed and if their water supply is always remembered.

[*Photographic Publications.*

A BIRD-EATING SPIDER OF THE AMAZON ABOUT TO POUNCE ON
TWO YOUNG BIRDS.

A TORPEDO ABOUT TO ENTER THE WATER. [*Crown Copyright.*

# HOW A TORPEDO WORKS?

A TORPEDO can be described as a huge, self-propelling explosive shell. It is like an elongated artillery shell in shape, and has a nose containing a detonator, which, on contact with an obstacle, fires a highly-explosive charge carried in the fore part of the body.

It contains a small, high-powered and high-speed engine worked by compressed air ; or by air expanded by the interaction of two chemicals. This engine drives two propellers at the stern of the torpedo. One rotates in one direction and the other in the other. If only one propeller were used, the effect would be to turn the propeller in one direction and the torpedo in the other, and little forward progress would be made.

The torpedo is launched from a special type of low-pressure gun, known as a torpedo tube, carried on a ship and adjustable for angles of fire so as to give the direction of the line of travel as the torpedo is propelled into the water. Afterwards, its forward motion is given by the engine inside and, to ensure that it does not deviate from its course, a gyroscope is fitted inside and driven by the engine. It keeps the torpedo from deflecting from its course, while an automatic horizontal rudder ensures that it shall travel on an even plane—

not diving and not rising—so as to be certain of striking its target just below the water line.

Once the torpedo is in the water, it moves steadily forward on its mission of destruction just below the surface of the water, for all the world like a miniature submarine. A white line of foam from its propellers darting out towards the object at which it is directed is the only indication of the torpedo's approach.

The nose or "war head" of the torpedo, containing the explosive, is detachable and is generally stowed away to prevent accidents. For practice purposes, this "war head" is replaced by a special dummy head, which, while resorting the weight and balance of the torpedo, is quite harmless.

Latest developments include the launching of torpedoes from seaplanes and their control by means of wireless. Torpedoes are still based on the original design of Robert Whitehead, who made the first effective torpedo in 1866.

*[Stephen Cribb.*

HOISTING A TORPEDO ABOARD AFTER A PRACTICE RUN.

# WHAT ARE THE TRADE WINDS?

THE Trade Winds are great air-currents each a thousand miles wide and over two thousand miles long which blow steadily towards the equator from a north-easterly direction in the northern hemisphere and from a south-easterly direction in the southern hemisphere. They are strong, very dry winds and parch the lands over which they pass. That is why most of the deserts of the world lie in the track of these remarkable winds. Their origin is also interesting. We have seen how the earth rotates fastest (at seventeen miles a minute) at the equator and does not rotate at all at the two poles.+ As they flow south towards the equator,† currents of cold air from the arctic regions cannot keep pace with the increasingly rapid rotation of the earth from west to east. They are thus deflected westwards; north winds become north-east winds. Exactly the same happens in the southern hemisphere. Air currents flowing equatorwards from the Antarctic regions are also deflected towards the west; south winds there become south-east winds. The Trade Winds, we see, are really produced by the earth's rotation.

+ See "*How Fast the Earth Rotates?*" page 78
† See "*What Causes Wind?*" page 212.

# WHAT FISH ARE KEPT AS SERVANTS?

TO find one such fish, we must go to the north-west coast of Madagascar, that large island off the south-east of Africa. There, a fish called *Hamby* is often caught. It is as long as a man's arm. It has a back fin just like a brush and on this there is a sticky liquid like gum. One old naturalist who knew that island well tells how it fastens upon another fish from below with this brush, and the captured fish is held fast. Needless to say, the people of the island make use of this fish. They catch it and put it in a wooden cage. This they fasten in the sea. Since it is a valuable thing, they feed it with rice or cassava, or small fish. It is a servant which is very useful. When they want it to get to work, they tie a long string round its tail and let the fish go, while they hold the string and follow in a canoe. As soon as it fastens upon a fish, the fishermen pull it in and take the fish it has caught for them.

THE MATTERHORN

This famous mountain is on the Swiss-Italian border, near the Swiss village of Zermatt, and is 14,780 feet high.    It
is the ambition of every mountaineer to climb it.

"BOMBING" INSECTS

This helicopter is spraying insecticide on mosquito larvæ in the water below. The chemical mixture is blown down
by the current of air from the rotor blades.

[B.O.A.C.

NIGERIAN EMIRS ARRIVING BY AIR AT LAGOS AIRPORT.

# TELL ME, PLEASE?

1. What is laughing gas?
2. What do we mean by Abracadabra?
3. Why do we call a sailor a " tar " ?
4. Where are the eyes of a snail?
5. What is the world's smallest bird?
6. What is a Whatnot?
7. What was the Holy Grail?
8. What are the colours of the spectrum?
9. What do the letters AB stand for?
10. What do we call the resting-place of a hare?
11. What is another name for ermine?
12. What animal fells trees?
13. What is the native home of the black swan?
14. What is the circumference of the world at the equator?

*Answers to these questions will be found on page 162.*

[Fox Photos.

AN INFRA-RED RAY PHOTOGRAPH OF ST. MICHAEL'S MOUNT, WITH
PENZANCE IN THE BACKGROUND.

# ANSWERS TO QUESTIONS on page 161

1. A gas that has an intoxicating effect when inhaled : nitrous oxide, used as an anaesthetic.

2. A mystical and occult word used as a charm.

3. Because his clothes and hands are usually smeared with the tar from the ship's tackle.

4. At the end of the two longest horns.

5. A humming bird.

6. A piece of furniture constructed to hold miscellaneous objects.

7. The cup said to have been used by Christ at the Last Supper

8. Indigo, Yellow, Orange, Red, Blue, Green and Violet.

9. Able Seaman, a sailor of the first class.

10. A form.

11. Stoat.

12. The beaver.

13. Southern Australia and Tasmania.

14. About 25,000 miles.

# WHAT ARE COSMIC RAYS?

COSMIC rays are identical in fundamental nature with radium rays, X-rays, ordinary visible light, unseen infra-red heat rays and wireless waves. They are one and all electro-magnetic waves and *differ only in size or wavelength,* just as little pond ripples and big Atlantic rollers are both water waves of vastly different size. Electric waves, like water waves, are carriers of energy, but, unlike water waves, the bigger they are the less energy they possess. The smaller the size of the waves (or the shorter their wavelength) the more powerful and penetrating they are. Wireless waves are the longest (biggest) electric waves and cosmic rays are the shortest (smallest).

Ordinary light cannot pass through even a thin sheet of brown paper, but X-rays, simply because they are about ten thousand times shorter, penetrate several inches of our flesh so that doctors are able to photograph the bones and internal organs of the human body.

Certain radium rays, being over twenty times shorter than X-rays, can penetrate three times as far into solid substances. They can pass through six inches of lead and on this account are highly dangerous to handle. Yet the whole earth is under a heavy and continual bombardment from cosmic rays which *pass clean through fifteen feet of solid lead*, because they are probably one hundred times shorter even than the most powerful radium rays, and measure *less than a millionth of a millionth part of an inch* long.

They are known as cosmic because they do not appear to come from the sun, moon, planets or stars, but from the outer, greater cosmos—the more distant, less-explored depths of the universe.

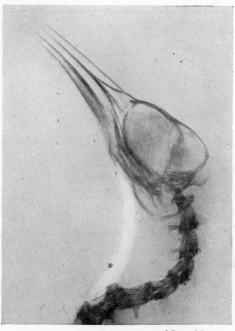

[*Central Press.*

AN X-RAY PHOTOGRAPH OF A PENGUIN'S HEAD AND NECK.

This picture shows how the spine is curved, which makes the neck very flexible and thus especially fitted to enable the bird to catch fish, its natural food.

# WHAT IS A DUST DEVIL?

YOU may have noticed how sometimes on a gusty day a puff of wind will swoop down on the dust lying in the road, twirl it into the air in a spiral, and then carry it along for some distance before letting it drop again. Dust Devils are similar happenings, but on a very much larger scale, and they are to be met with in the open desert spaces of Asia and Africa. They often occur on the plains of India and the native name for them is " Bagoola." These pillars of dust or sand are sometimes one thousand feet in height and move across the ground at a great rate in a similar fashion to water-spouts at sea. The unfortunate travellers who encounter one of these perils of the desert are liable to be overwhelmed and suffocated, and stories are told of entire caravans being blotted out, never to be seen again save for the discovery, many years later, of a heap of bones which a contrary wind has uncovered. Hence it is not surprising that such a gruesome name as Dust Devil should have been bestowed on these cyclones, and one can understand how the superstition arose that they were indeed evil spirits seeking to destroy the rash mortals who had dared to venture into their territory.

Sir Richard Burton, the celebrated traveller and explorer, mentions that the phenomenon is often to be seen in Arabia, and is referred to in the " Arabian Nights " which he translated into English. One of these stories tells of a merchant who accidentally kills the son of a Jinnee, or evil spirit, by throwing away a date stone, and in consequence is condemned to death by the enraged father. However, he is granted a year's respite in order to wind up his affairs, and then returns to the fatal spot to meet his doom. The story goes on to relate how, as he waited, " the dust was agitated, and became an enormous pillar, approaching from the middle of the desert ; and this dust subsided, and behold, the Jinnee, with a drawn sword in his hand ; his eyes casting forth sparks of fire." One is glad to remember that the story has a happy ending after all, and certainly it helps us to understand the dread inspired by these sudden and dangerous storms.

In Australia, too, the natives believe that the terrifying and immense columns of twirling red sand which pass rapidly across the desert are evil spirits, and a traveller relates how a black youth ran after one of them in order to kill it with his boomerang. After

## A SANDSTORM IN THE DESERT.

" Dust-Devil " is the name often applied to the whirling columns of sand that in Arabia, North Africa, and other desert regions will sometimes descend on the traveller with appalling suddenness, even when the sky is blue and cloudless. They sweep along at a terrific rate and with deadly fury, sucking up every article in their path. For man and camel alike the only hope is to lie prostrate on the ground until the worst is over.

some time he returned very weary, saying he had killed the demon, who, however, in his anger at being pursued, had growled at him and consequently he also must die shortly. With such a belief so widely spread among primitive races, it is easy to understand how the name Dust Devil has persisted.

# WHAT INSECTS "KEEP COWS"?

THE aphis is a tiny insect which spends its life in taking into its body sap from the plants upon which it lives. It makes a kind of honey or honey-dew which those wonderful creatures the ants want for their food. There are any number of these aphides, and there would be far more if they had not enemies like the ladybird. The ants might be content to get their honey as they need it ; they have only to tap the aphis on the side of its abdomen, and the honey drops out for them. But they are not content to do this. They keep the aphides as human beings keep cows. Some even make stalls for them at the place where they are feeding on plants. Others carry them into their own

[H. Bastin.

ANTS TENDING GREENFLY.

nest, where they keep them with every care. This gives them what they need, a steady supply of their honey-dew. It is not a hardship for the aphides that they have their ants like a body-guard about them. They keep away from them other enemies, and while the ants protect them, they are safe.

Some kinds of ants make out of bark and grasses a covering for their "cows." It is a building with a dome, and a doorway which is guarded by one or two sentinels. If we were to make an opening in these shelters, the ants would seize their "cows" and carry them away to another place of safety. All this seems wonderful, but there seems nothing too wonderful to expect from the ants, who are a little people, but very clever.

# WHAT IS AN UMBRELLA BIRD?

TO find the umbrella-bird, we should have to travel to the plains of the Amazon, but even if we made that journey, we might miss this shy bird. It lives in the higher branches of the trees, and since its food is chiefly wild fruit, it does not need to come into the open.

It gets its name from the crest, which looks much like the plumes which used to be on the top of a soldier's helmet. This consists of straight feathers, the ends of which curve outwards. This bird has also long feathers going downwards from the throat and neck, making what looks like a loose muffler; this has a steely-blue appearance, but the male bird looks deep black in colour. The female bird has nothing like the full crest, and is much duller in appearance.

The Indians call this bird the fife-bird because of its peculiar notes. It can be heard when it is not seen. One traveller who both heard it and saw it tells how the bird spread out widely its umbrella crest, waved its steely-blue fold under its beak, and bowing its head slowly forward, uttered a loud piping note; and he could tell that the Indians had not given it a wrong name. If we want the name of the family to which it belongs, we shall remember it best as the family of Chatterers, many of which are curious in appearance, others being gorgeous in colour. Should you ever wish to look this bird up in an encyclopædia, the scientific name of its genus is *Cephaloptesus*.

# HOW AN ESCALATOR WORKS?

WITHOUT doubt, the most popular and fascinating wonder of all the wonders of the Underground Tube Railway of today, for boys and girls, at any rate, are the moving stairs or escalators as they are properly called.

When the first tube railways were constructed, escalators for passengers were not thought of and the public used lifts in which to travel up and down between the underground stations and the streets, and these lifts still remain on some of the older lines. With the ever-increasing numbers of the travelling public, particularly during the business rush hours, it was soon recognized that lifts, even a battery of lifts, at many stations, were hopelessly inadequate to cope with the continually growing congestion.

And so the escalators were introduced, and we now find them in use on all new tube railways and extensions.

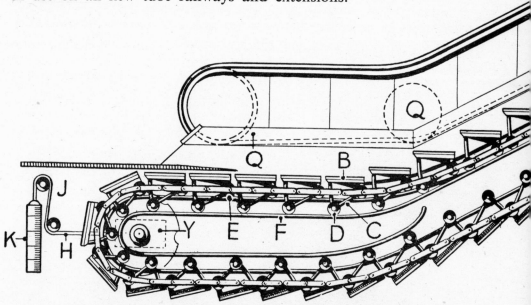

An escalator is an endless chain of steps which passes over a drive roller X, on the level at the top, down an incline, along the level at the bottom, round a bottom roller Y and up again to the top roller.

Chains A (one on each side) carry the steps B, hinged at the back of each step to a link hinge of the chain. Triangular struts C below each step carry rollers D, which keep their treads always horizontal. This is done by means of guide rails E and F, which engage with rollers at the point where the step is hinged to the chain ; and other guide rails F, which engage with the rollers at the bottom of the struts C.

When the steps are travelling on the level, the two rails E and F are at a distance apart which keeps the steps horizontal. As the steps approach the incline at the point G, these rails F converge to the same line as the rails E, so that the struts end of the step is

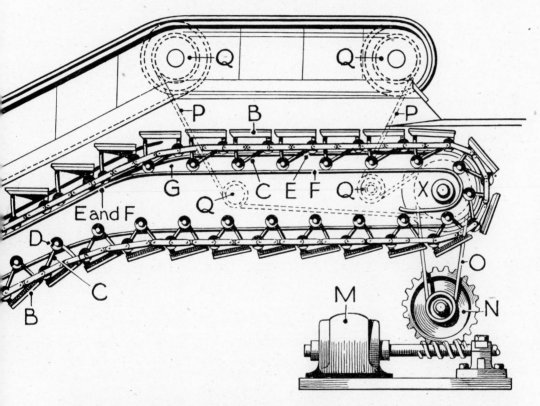

pushed up and the step keeps horizontal but at an angle with the chain, now inclined. The chains are kept taut by a cable pulley, and weight H, J and K, which pulls the bottom roller of chain A along a slide. The travelling rubber hand grip L, on each side hand rail, travels at the same speed as the steps ; all being driven by an electric motor M, which is geared by worm and wheel N and a chain O to the top drive roller X. The rollers on the chain engage in hollow spaces in the edge of the rollers X and Y. The hand rail L is driven by the belt P and the pulleys Q from the drive roller X.

# WHAT IS A BARKING TOAD?

YOU have all heard a dog bark, but how many of you have heard a toad bark? Frogs and toads of all kinds make extraordinary croaking sounds, particularly during the spring months. The Bull Frog of Canada is reputed to possess the loudest croaking abilities, making its voice heard miles away.

During the breeding season toads are quite as noisy as frogs. One of the largest of the toads is the Barking Toad, also known as the Ornamental Horned Toad, which is to be found in parts of South America. This toad, which is shown in our illustration below, has a very poisonous bite and sometimes, when it gets the chance, makes a meal of young ducklings and baby chickens, frequenting farmyards and poultry farms for this purpose.

Farmers keep a sharp look out for the Barking Toad as it is a nasty customer to tackle. It has horn-like upper eyelids and is about eight inches in length, normally, but has the power to puff itself out to an enormous size, as if about to burst. When attacked, it emits a series of sharp, harsh croaks, exactly like the bark of a dog. Its venom is highly poisonous and it is said to be capable of killing a horse.

When breeding, the Barking Toad is to be found in pools and marshy creeks, its noisy notes, somewhat like those of a wind instrument interspersed with wailing sounds which may be mistaken for a child crying, are heard for a good distance.

Our own British Toad, as many of you know, has a gland of strong-smelling liquid on its head, which it squirts out when at bay.

By courtesy of]                    [Carl Hagenbeck.
A BRAZILIAN HORNED OR BARKING TOAD.

*By courtesy of*]        [*The Commonwealth of Australia.*

### KOOKABURRA OR LAUGHING JACKASS.

This Australian bird belongs to the same family as our Kingfisher and takes its name from the fact that its call can easily be mistaken for someone laughing.

171

# WHAT IS THE GREAT BARRIER REEF?

IF you look at the map of Australia (which is both the smallest continent and the largest island in the world), you will find the Great Barrier Reef stretching along the upper portion of the eastern coast-line.

It extends for over twelve hundred miles and it is the largest continuous coral reef in the world.

The openings that occur in the reef are found opposite the river mouths, and it has been suggested that these gaps have been worn by the fresh water flowing from these rivers, but this seems unlikely as the distance from the shore to these breaks in the reef varies from thirty to ninety miles. More probably these channels are due to the subsistence of the land beneath the sea.

Between the Barrier Reef and the mainland is a passage known as " Grand Canal," and the ships trading along the coast make use of this sheltered fairway and thus escape the formidable breakers which beat perpetually on the outer edge of the reef.

[E.N.A.

A VIEW OF THE CRESCENT REEF ON THE OUTER BARRIER, QUEENSLAND.

[*Aerofilms, Ltd.*

### THE TAJ MAHAL, AGRA, INDIA.

This beautiful building of glistening white marble is the tomb of the Queen of the Emperor Shah Jehan. It dates from 1640, and tradition declares that the gifted architect was cast from the top to ensure that he should never design another building to rival it.

# TELL ME, PLEASE?

1. Whence do we get Chinchilla fur?
2. What do we mean by treasure trove?
3. What is the origin of our word " Admiral "?
4. What is asbestos?
5. How many stripes does the American flag contain?
6. What and where is the highest lake in the world?
7. Whence does the expression " Tally-Ho " originate?
8. What planet in the solar system is nearest to the sun?
9. What is a cordwainer?
10. How do peanuts grow?
11. What is the highest mountain in Europe?
12. What makes the moon shine?
13. What is the origin of the term " Rotten Row "?

*For answers to these questions, see page* 174.

# ANSWERS TO QUESTIONS on page 173

1. From a small South American rodent with pale grey fur.

2. Money, treasure and similar valuables found in the earth of unknown ownership.

3. From *Amir*, the Arabic for " Commander."

4. An incombustible fibrous mineral.

5. Thirteen.

6. Lake Titicaca in Bolivia.

7. From the French *Il est allé-Oh !* meaning " gone away ! "

8. Mercury.

9. A shoemaker.

10. In the earth on the root of a plant.

11. Mont Blanc.

12. The reflection of the rays from the sun.

13. From the French *Route du Roi*, meaning The King's Drive.

[B.O.A.C.

**WINDSOR CASTLE FROM THE AIR.**

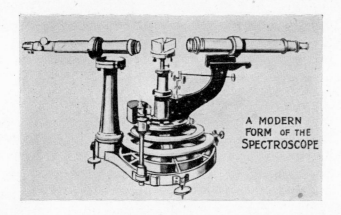

A MODERN FORM OF THE SPECTROSCOPE

# WHAT A SPECTROSCOPE DOES?

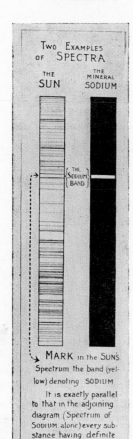

Two Examples of SPECTRA

THE SUN        THE MINERAL SODIUM

(THE SODIUM BAND)

↘ MARK in the Sun's Spectrum the band (yellow) denoting SODIUM

It is exactly parallel to that in the adjoining diagram (Spectrum of Sodium alone) every substance having definite & unalterable place (or places) common to all spectra in which it occurs

A SPECTROSCOPE is the scientist's rainbow maker. We most of us know that white light is really made up of lights of many different colours. What a spectroscope does is to sort out any kind of light into all the different wavelengths of which it is blended. This would not in itself be particularly useful if the wavelength of light had not got a good deal to tell us about the source from which it comes.

Any chemical element, for examples iron or oxygen, when it is heated sufficiently strongly, emits only light of a large number of particular wavelengths. Once these wavelengths have been measured, a spectroscope can, therefore, be used as an analytical instrument. Knowing that such-and-such wave lengths are present in light, we can say at once that such-and-such chemical elements must be present in its source. It is in this way that astronomers can tell what the stars are made of.

From the extent to which the known pattern of lines is displaced to one side or the other, it is also possible to tell how fast the light source in question is moving towards or away from us. It is in this way that we can tell that the universe as a whole is expanding.

# WHY STRIKING A MATCH MAKES IT LIGHT?

WHEN a native rubs two sticks together to light a fire, he is applying the same principle as we do when we strike a match. Friction produces heat, and a sufficient amount of heat causes fire. The only difference is that a match head and the striking surface of the box form an inflammable mixture. It consists of phosphorus and chlorate of potash, the latter being equivalent to a concentrated supply of oxygen. In a non-safety match the complete mixture is on the match head, and so the match will strike on any surface that is rough enough to provide sufficient friction.

# WHAT ARE BOYS AND GIRLS MADE OF?

LIVING flesh and blood possessing power to grow, move, think and speak. Their bodies are composed of millions of microscopical " cells," called " protoplasm," arranged so as to make : a " framework " of bone, " muscles " to move the frame, organs to digest food and, through the " blood," nourish other parts, organs to take in air and extract the " oxygen " which the body *must* have, organs to get rid of used-up material, and an organ to think, remember, receive impressions and give orders to the body, also a " soul " or " spirit " which nobody can see or define.

# HOW FAST YOUR BRAIN WORKS?

IF someone pricks you with a pin, you say, " Oh ! "
In the interval between the " prick " and the " Oh ! " the sense of " touch " has passed the " feeling " to the brain, the brain has decided that it is a sudden " pain," and passes an order to your breathing muscles and organ of speech and you make a sound. The " current " which conveys these messages and produces the effect of " Oh ! " travels at about one hundred and twenty-five yards per second. Other " time " reactions take about as follows : sight, one-fifth second ; hearing, one-seventh second ; touch, a little less. Complicated " thinking " takes longer, of course.

SEVERAL SKYSCRAPERS IN NEW YORK HAVE FIFTY OR MORE STOREYS.

**THE GREAT METEOR CRATER, ARIZONA.**
It is 600 feet deep and nearly three miles in circumference.

**A BUSY SCENE IN THE OCEAN DOCK, SOUTHAMPTON.**
In the background can be seen the great floating dock and a giant floating crane.

[*Topical.*

## SEA-SHELLS.

1 and 3. Murex.
2. Pterocera.
4. Harpa (the Harp).
5. Spondylus (Thorny Oyster).
6. Dolium.
7. Tridacna (Giant Clam).
8. Voluta.
9. Strombus (Wing-shell).
10 and 15. Conus (Cone shells).

11. Thedoxis.
12. and 14. Nerita.
13. Cypraea (Cowry).
16. Cassis (Helmet-shell).
17. Meleagrina.
18. Pecten (Scallop)
19. Solen (Razor-shell).
20. Cardium (Cockle).

179

# DO CRABS CLIMB TREES?

CRABS as we know them live by the sea ; but in some parts of the world, in India or in the West Indies, for example, there are land crabs which live two or three miles from the sea. But when the time comes for the females to lay their eggs, they move together to the sea, where the eggs are laid. It is said that when this time comes nothing stands in the way of these crabs. They come out of their sheltered homes under the rocks or in hollow trees, or in holes, and in a long line perhaps a mile long. The males lead the way and go in a straight line ; they do not go round the thing which is in their way, but they climb over it, whether it is a hedge or a tree or a church or a cliff. If there is danger in the straight way, they take it none the less. We talk of going in this way as making a " bee-line " ; it might be said as truly that those who take the shortest way are making a " land crab line." When they reach the sea, the eggs are laid, and the young crabs arrive. This is in the spring ; but when the summer comes, the crabs return to their burrows, close up the openings, and there wait till the old shell is cast and the new one is ready. The most notorious tree-climber, however, is the Purse-crab, a large land species, also known as the Robber-crab and the Coconut-crab. It lives on fruit, especially

[Neville Kingston.

**A LAND CRAB.**
The land crabs of tropical countries are terrestrial and air-breathing.

[F. W. Bond.

**A ROBBER OR COCONUT-CRAB.**
A crab of the Hermit group, which climbs palm trees to get the coco-nuts.

coconuts, which it climbs the palms to obtain and cracks the nuts quite easily with its powerful pincers. This giant crab, which sometimes weighs as much as twenty pounds, is related to the Hermit-crabs. It is a native of Ceylon, Mauritius and the tropical islands of the Pacific and Indian Oceans.

# WHAT IS THE WILL-O'-THE-WISP?

WILL-O'-THE-WISP, called also *ignis fatuus* and Jack o' Lantern, is in the strict scientific sense just burning methane, a colourless, odourless gas, better known as the deadly fire-damp of the coal mines. The gas is given off by wet, decaying vegetable matter, and so is often met with over swamps, mires and peat-bogs. When ignited it burns with a flickering, luminous flame that is said to have lured many curious travellers to a slow, agonising death in the black, slimy depths of a bog. Hence the word is often used to denote anything elusive or misleading.

# HOW A MOTOR CAR'S PRESELECTOR GEAR WORKS?

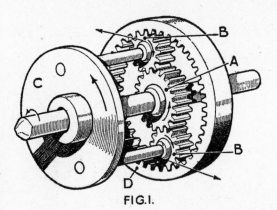

FIG.I.

WITH a preselector gear box, the car driver selects the gear he next requires to use by means of a small lever on the centre of the steering wheel (figure 4). He does this before he actually makes the change, which is done by depressing the clutch pedal. The gears are epicyclic (figure 1)—a gear for each forward speed (except top direct) and reverse. They are (figure 2): B reverse, C first forward, D second, E third; while a cone clutch F locks all these together and gives the direct top gear, when all the gears rotate together and the rear axle driving-shaft, A, is driven by the engine shaft G at its own speed.

One of the epicyclic gears is shown at figure 1. A brake holds a toothed ring D. The engine drives the sun wheel A and the planet wheels (pivoted on plate C) move round the annular teeth and drive C in the same direction but at a reduced speed. If C is held, the planet wheels are driven round on their bearings by the sun wheel and rotate the toothed ring D in a reverse direction.

Various sizes of gear wheels in the four trains give various speeds. So that brakes indicated by letters H, I, J and K and the clutch F in the diagram (figure 2) can control all four speeds and reverse.

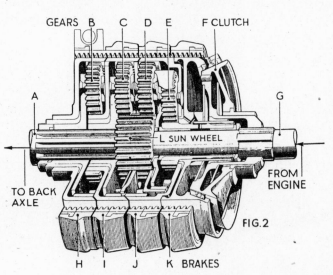

FIG.2

182

# HOW A PRESELECTOR GEAR WORKS?

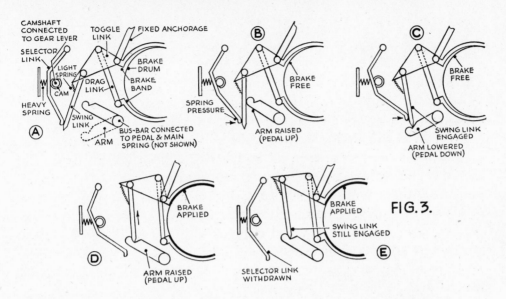

FIG. 3.

The brake bands on all are operated by the driver's pedal, which pushes up a swing link on a toggle which closes the brake on one of the drums.

The different movements are shown in figure 3. At A a selector link is kept pressed by a spring to a cam on a shaft (a cam for each gear) which the selecting lever on the steering wheel moves round. At A the gear brake is free. At B the cam has allowed the selector link to come forward. At C the driver's pedal lowers the arm and the selector link presses the swing link into the slot at the end of the pedal arm. At D the driver releases the pedal and the pedal arm rises, pushes up the spring link and pulls the brake on—applying the gear by holding the gear drum. At E the cam has returned the selector link.

The cams which work the gears are on a cam shaft which is moved round to bring different cams (for different gears) into position by a quadrant and a lever—the latter connected to the driver's gear selecting lever on the steering wheel (figure 4). The preselector gear described above is of the type fitted on Armstrong-Siddeley cars.

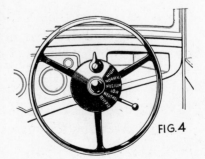

FIG. 4

# HOW WE MEASURE THE SIZE AND WEIGHT OF THE STARS?

ASTRONOMERS are able to weigh the stars because of the same fundamental law of nature that enables us to weigh ourselves or a grocer to weigh a pound of tea.

Weight is simply the consequence of the gravitational attraction or pull which exists between all bodies throughout the universe. In everyday life we weigh things by measuring the earth's gravitational pull upon them with the help of a device such as a spring balance or a pair of scales. Here, only the earth's pull counts, because we are actually on and in physical contact with the earth. All bodies attract one another, however.

It is mainly the gravitational pull of the moon on the earth which raises the ocean tides, and the stronger gravitational pull of the earth keeps the moon revolving round the earth quite as effectively as if a gigantic steel rod connected them. The earth's pull prevents the moon running off into space and the speed of the moon (2,300 miles an hour) in its orbit saves the moon from being pulled on to the earth and colliding.

The law of gravitation shows that the speeds with which bodies revolve round other bodies depends only upon their distance apart and their mass (weight) or the total quantity of material contained in them.

As practically every star, nebula, and system of stars in space is rotating and revolving, and as the spectroscope (and other methods) can tell us their orbital speeds, we can literally weigh and measure the stars.

# WHERE ASPHALT COMES FROM?

IT is little more than a hundred years since asphalt was first used in England for paving roads and footways and in building operations, but the substance was known to the ancients. The " slime " used as mortar by the builders of the Tower of Babel was a kind of asphalt, and the mother of Moses employed a similar material to waterproof the cradle in which she placed her infant son before hiding him among the rushes of the Nile. It was a species of asphalt, too, that the Egyptians made use of to preserve their mummies.

# WHERE ASPHALT COMES FROM ?

This sticky, semi-solid substance is found in many parts of the world, including Switzerland, Belgium, the Dead Sea and the U.S.A., but the main source of supply nowadays, and from which the best quality is obtained, is the " Pitch Lake," the crater of an extinct volcano, at La Brea in the south-west corner of the West Indian island of Trinidad. It covers an area of a hundred acres—nearly three times the size of the Zoological Gardens. Although one

[*Keystone.*

Removing pitch from the famous Devil's Cauldron, a lake of asphalt, Trinidad, British West Indies. No sooner is a layer of pitch removed than more is forced to the surface.

hundred and fifty thousand tons are removed every year, there are no signs of the supply being exhausted. The top layer of the asphalt hardens on coming into contact with the air, and is broken up with picks and removed ; then the softer layer beneath rises and solidifies in turn, and the process is repeated.

Asphalt is a Greek word meaning " of foreign or strange origin," and even today we are uncertain how it is formed. At one time it was believed to be derived from decayed vegetable matter, but the theory is now held that probably it is the result of the oxidization and evaporation of the liquid petroleum which is present in the land surrounding the asphalt deposits.

# DO FISH CLIMB TREES?

IF a fish climbs trees, we may be sure of two things : it would not do such a difficult thing if it were not in search of food, and it would not be able to do it if it had not specially strong fins.

A fish which does climb trees at times is called the *Mud-skipper* or *Walking-fish* ; and if we wanted to find it most easily, we should go to Malaya. When the tides go out, it does not go with them, but rolls about in the mud as if it enjoyed it and were having a game. For a fish in the mud it can move quickly. With its fins, which are like arms well forward under its great eyes, and not like the fins which are meant only for swimming, it moves along ; the fins draw the body half an inch at each step. But since the insects which it wants for food can be found on the tree, it uses the same powerful fins to draw it up the trunk. We are accustomed when we look into a tree to see birds and squirrels, but we should think it an unusual thing if we saw the big, staring eyes of the Mud-skipper looking down on us. We may see them if we ever go into the tropics.

Another fish which ascends trees at times is the *Anabas* or *Climbing Perch*, found in rivers and ponds in the East Indies. It is a spiny, perch-like fish, about six inches in length. It uses its spiny gill-coves and anal fin, together with its power of distending and contracting its body, in its mode of progression. It has been established that this fish is capable of existing out of water for days and can travel overland for some distance.

[*W. S. Berridge.*

WALKING-FISH, OR MUD-SKIPPER.

This is truly a " fish out of water " for it spends more time out of water than in it, and if placed in deep water is quickly drowned ! It climbs roots and banks by means of the breast fins. The walking-fish is a member of the Goby family, and is common in the rivers of West Africa and Burma.

A SKYLARK SOARING.

[*Harold Bastin.*

# HOW FAST DO BIRDS FLY?

IN days before there were telephones or wireless, news was often carried by homing pigeons. It is said that the news of the Battle of Waterloo was brought to London in this way. These birds are not by any means the fastest, but they have a wonderful way of coming back home. Their speed is said to be something over thirty miles an hour. The swift lives up to its name and travels at about seventy-five miles an hour. It can exceed this speed on occasion and travel at as much as a hundred miles an hour. It is not so much the swiftness of the birds that astonishes us but the long distances which they cover. Linnets which have lived in England in the summer may be found in Natal during the winter.

Taking all our birds into consideration, their average speed is about forty-five miles an hour. Small perching birds fly between twenty-five and forty miles an hour ; such birds as the crows, magpies and rooks, from thirty-five to forty-five miles an hour ; the starling nearly fifty miles an hour ; geese over fifty, and ducks nearly sixty miles an hour. Flying with the wind, of course, their speed is greatly increased, while against it the pace is proportionately decreased.

# THE KINGS AND QUEENS OF ENGLAND

*(From the Norman Conquest to the Present Day.)*

## THE NORMAN PERIOD

1066 William I.
1087 William II.

1100 Henry I.
1135 Stephen.

## THE PLANTAGENET PERIOD

1154 Henry II.
1189 Richard I.
1199 John.
1216 Henry III.
1272 Edward I.
1307 Edward II.
1327 Edward III.

1377 Richard II.
1399 Henry IV.
1413 Henry V.
1422 Henry VI.
1461 Edward IV.
1483 Edward V.
1483 Richard III.

## THE TUDOR PERIOD

1485 Henry VII.
1509 Henry VIII.
1547 Edward VI.

1553 Jane.
1553 Mary I.
1558 Elizabeth I.

## THE STUART PERIOD

1603 James I.
1625 Charles I.
1649 Commonwealth.
1660 Charles II.

1685 James II.
1689 William and Mary.
1702 Anne.

## THE HANOVERIAN PERIOD

1714 George I.
1727 George II.
1760 George III.
1820 George IV.

1830 William IV.
1837 Victoria.
1901 Edward VII.

## THE WINDSOR PERIOD

1910 George V.
1936 Edward VIII.

1936 George VI.
1952 Elizabeth II.

[*Newton & Co., Ltd.*

**THE ROYAL THRONES IN THE HOUSE OF LORDS, WESTMINSTER.**

189

AN ORANG-UTAN'S NEST IN A TREE. [W. S. Berridge.

# WHAT LARGE ANIMALS BUILD NESTS IN TREES?

EVERYBODY knows that most birds build their nests in trees. Some of them construct nests of enormous size, as we have already shown in our article on the Australian Brush Turkey, whose nest sometimes weighs as much as five tons ; but not so many people know that certain large animals actually build nests in the trees in much the same manner as birds.

The orang-utan, for example, one of the largest and most powerful of the apes and a native of Sumatra and Borneo, is a regular nest-builder and invariably erects quite a large nest-like platform of sticks high up in the trees for sleeping purposes. A large orang-utan, which somehow managed to gain its liberty at the London Zoo, some little time back, built the nest shown in the above illustration in a single night.

The gorilla, the largest and most powerful of all the apes, also builds a sort of structure or arbour in the trees, and this is made especially secure and an extra comfortable nest provided when a young gorilla is expected.

The chimpanzee, too, perhaps the most intelligent of all the apes, constructs a large and cosy nest in the trees, the male chimpanzee usually sleeping underneath the nest on guard over his family.

Quite a number of the smaller monkeys and lemurs build nests. And always because these creatures are safest in the trees.

*From the Paramount Film]* ["*Rango*".

### AN ORANG-UTAN AT HOME.

The hair of this ape is long and reddish-chestnut in colour. It uses its long arms to pass from branch to branch with great rapidity.

191

BLOWING BUBBLES.

[*Fox Photos.*

# WHY A SOAP BUBBLE SHOWS SO MANY HUES?

THE varied colours of a soap bubble are one proof that light consists of waves, not unlike those of the sea. It is one of the characteristics of waves that two sets of waves can " interfere " with one another. For example, if two stones are dropped close together into a pond, the crest of one set of waves will in some places be reinforced by the crests of the second set, and in other places be cancelled out. So it is with light, and a thin film, such as that of a soap bubble, provides a peculiarly beautiful illustration of the way in which this happens. Light can be reflected either from the front surface of the film or from the back surface, and if the film is very thin, the two sets of waves will interfere. Whether the two sets of waves will reinforce or cancel out in any particular direction will, obviously, depend on the distance between successive light ripples ; that is, on the wavelength or colour of the light. So it is that an observer looking at a soap bubble sees all manner of different colours. It is for the same reason that thin films of oil on a wet road appear many coloured, and the same effect can sometimes be seen on the sea on a larger scale.

# WHAT BIRD USES A NEEDLE AND THREAD?

IT is difficult to point to anything man has invented to which no analogue, or parallel, may be found in the natural world.

Long before man appeared on the earth, tailors were busy plying their " needle " and thread. The " needle " then used was not a manufactured article, for it is only man that invents working tools.

Nevertheless, the working principle was the same, for it punctured holes, applied threads, and stitched materials. It was the beak of the Tailor Bird of India—a small, wren-like bird, but of a greenish colour.

This familiar little bird of the East constructs a very cleverly-built nest. Selecting a shrub with large leaves, it pierces holes more or less irregularly down each side of one of the leaves.

It then obtains a thread of silk from the cocoon of some silk-weaving caterpillar, or it may be from a spider's web, or even strands of vegetable fibre.

Provided with such material, it then constructs a long thread, often much longer than is required, by joining the strands together. When the thread is made, it proceeds to stitch the margins of the leaf neatly together through the pierced holes.

[E. N. A.
A TAILOR BIRD ABOUT TO ENTER ITS NEST.

The leaf then forms a kind of hollowed cone, but, should it not be large enough, two, or even three leaves may be stitched together in the same manner.

The bird then gathers a quantity of soft cotton-wool material to form a cosy nest for its eggs within the attached leaves.

The nest is usually built amongst the lower branches, and is well concealed amidst the ordinary leaves of the shrub.

Although one of the commonest small birds of India, and one that seeks man's habitations, its nest is rarely found.

A YOUNG SIAMESE COOLIE LAYING OUT BRUSH TWIGS TO DRY
IN A BANGKOK STREET.

# WHAT IS A PORTUGUESE MAN-O'-WAR?

THE name is given to two different things, which are very closely related. There is a jelly-fish, large and strange in shape, which is so called; it has what looks like an air-bladder on the surface of the water; below in the water long feelers hang downward, and have the power to sting horribly anyone who touches them. It is a most beautiful jelly-fish, but sailors know better than to touch it.

But there is one kind of the fishes called rudder-fishes which enters into a partnership with this lovely but dangerous jelly-fish; and for this reason it has got the same name. It lodges with it. For fishes have two great ideas, they want to eat, and they want to escape being eaten. This rudder-fish therefore takes safe lodgings with the jelly-fish which can protect itself and others from enemies. Perhaps the jelly-fish knows nothing about all this; and the rudder-fish runs the risk of touching one of the batteries of stings. It does not look as if the rudder-fish gave anything in return, but we never know.

# HOW A GRASSHOPPER HEARS?

JUST how a grasshopper hears depends on the kind of grasshopper in question. The long-horned grasshoppers, together with the cricket, have ears in the "knees" of their fore legs. These ears consist of two external openings on opposite sides of each fore leg, with a thin membrane extended between them, the latter serving as a tympanum, or sounding drum. In the case of the short-horned grasshoppers, the ears are similar structures with somewhat crescent-shaped openings, but are situated on each side of the first body ring, just behind the thorax.

Since insects have their nerve centres generally distributed over the length of their bodies, and do not possess a brain, or main nerve centre, we need not necessarily look for ears on their head.

[Harold Bastin.

A MEADOW GRASSHOPPER CLINGING TO A GRASS STEM.

# WHY SOME ANIMALS MOVE ABOUT BY NIGHT AND SLEEP BY DAY?

IN the Bible we are told that in the night " all the beasts of the forest do creep forth," ; and the ancient singer adds " the young lions roar after their prey " ; but, " when the sun ariseth, they gather themselves together and lay them down in their dens."

There is no doubt that while some birds of prey move about in the day, the beasts of prey—lions, tigers, leopards, are awake at

A FLASHLIGHT PHOTOGRAPH OF A BADGER ON THE PROWL.

night, and sleep in the day. The reason is as the singer tells us, they go forth at night, simply because it is easier for them to hunt the other creatures upon which they live. They have eyes which can see more in the darkness than human beings can ; they can see, but since they move in the night, they are partly hidden from their prey, who cannot see so well by night as the beasts of prey. By day such animals as lions and tigers would have far more difficulty in catching their prey, which is probably very keen-sighted and fleet of foot. Travellers in Africa by night-time looking into the dark forests through which their road runs, can often see bright eyes and nothing more ; they know that the wild creatures are awake, seeing while they are not seen.

*By courtesy of*] [*South African Railways and Harbours.*

A GLIMPSE OF A KOODOO.

*From the Film*] [*" Africa Speaks ".*

LIONS AT THE KILL.

197

# WHY LAKES NEVER FREEZE SOLID?

FISH have every reason to be grateful for one peculiarity of water. Most liquids expand progressively as they are heated, as the mercury of a thermometer bulb expands when the thermometer is placed in the mouth. Water is an exception. If water is slowly heated, starting from 0 degrees Centigrade, the freezing point of water, it starts by contracting. At 4 degrees Centigrade water is at its heaviest, and only after that does it begin to expand. In cold weather fishes owe their lives to this peculiarity. In the ordinary way warm water is lighter than cold and tends to rise to the surface. But water on the point of freezing is lighter than water at 4 degrees. The result is that, as a lake is cooled in a cold spell, the coldest water rises to the surface. As ice is also lighter than water, this also remains on the surface. Taken together, these arrangements effectively prevent even cooling through the whole depth of the water. It is, therefore, rare for even a pond to freeze entirely solid, while lakes never do so. This is only one of many ways in which the physical properties of water seem to have been almost deliberately designed to help life as much as possible. It is no accident that we and all living things are largely made of it.

LAKE MICHIGAN DURING A SEVERE WINTER.

A POLAR BEAR AT PLAY.                    [*Keystone.*

# TELL ME, PLEASE?

1. Whence do we get the expression " to knuckle under "?
2. What do we mean by the " calibre " of a gun?
3. What is a dhow?
4. Why was the victor of Poitiers called " The Black Prince "?
5. What are the three primary colours?
6. Who was called " The Lady of the Lamp "?
7. What was the date of the compilation of the Doomsday Book?
8. What is the Equinox?
9. When is Empire Day?
10. What is a nautical knot?
11. What do we call the Pope's palace?
12. By what name are the Yeomen of the Guard usually called?
13. Who were the Vikings?

*Answers to these questions will be found on page* 200.

# ANSWERS TO QUESTIONS on page 199

1. From the game of marbles.
2. The diameter of the bore.
3. An Arab vessel with one or two masts.
4. Because he always wore black armour
5. Red, yellow and blue.
6. Florence Nightingale.
7. Between 1085 and 1086.
8. March 21st or September 21st, when the days and nights are of equal duration.
9. May 24th.
10. A measure of speed, equalling one and one-sixth statute miles per hour
11. The Vatican.
12. Beefeaters.
13. Sea rovers from Scandinavia.

[Dorien Leigh, Chase.

YOUNG TURTLES HATCHING OUT.

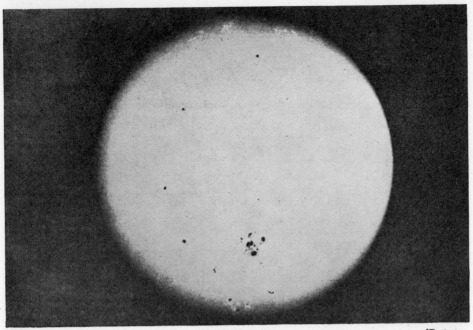

SUNSPOTS.

[*Topical.*

# WHAT ARE SUNSPOTS?

SUNSPOTS are to be seen as little black dots, or, when clustered together, as ink-like splashes on the sun's disc. They look black simply because they are only half as hot and bright as the rest of the sun's surface. Nevertheless, sunspots are *actually* as dazzling as limelight and nearly three times hotter than molten metal in a Bessemer blast furnace. They are of enormous size. This earth of ours could fall into one of the larger ones and be lost as easily as a pebble thrown into a pond. Recent research proves them to be furious revolving storms or tornadoes caused by terrific internal explosions, and into which huge clouds of glowing hydrogen and other gases are often sucked at speeds of over sixty miles a second. Though we now know what they are, we still do not know how they come to be biggest and most numerous every eleven years or so. There are many close and very curious connections between sunspots and the earth. Space permits us to mention here but two. The lovely coloured lights of the aurora borealis in the northern night sky are most brilliant when the sun is most spotted every eleven years. Hot, dry summers and cool, moist ones come and go in the same eleven year cycles.

## THE LEANING TOWER OF PISA.

Built in the thirteenth century, the tower is fourteen feet out of the perpendicular, having subsided when near completion. From it Galileo made his famous experiments to prove that falling bodies, great or small, descend with equal velocity.

# WHY A CLOCK PENDULUM SWINGS?

A PENDULUM swings by the force of gravity, and, theoretically, should swing for ever. Actually, friction and air resistance result in the swing becoming of less amplitude, although for a given length of pendulum it is always the same in time. This fact is used in the clock pendulum. The pendulum does not *work* the clock, but because it swings at a constant time, it regulates the movement. In the case of a clock, the pendulum is kept going by impulses from the spring or in the case of old-fashioned " grandfathers " by the fall of the weights. Since it is the length of the pendulum that decides the time it takes to make a swing or beat, moving the weight a little down makes the clock go slower and moving it up makes it move faster.

# DO OYSTERS GROW ON TREES?

THE answer to this question depends on what we mean by " growing " on trees. Oysters do not grow on trees in the same way that apples or pears do, but they are found on certain trees which grow in salt marshes and on the edge of tidal estuaries in the tropics of both the New and the Old Worlds. These trees are called Mangroves, and they send down roots into the nearby water, and to these roots the oysters, known as Mangrove Oysters, fasten themselves. The Mangroves grow very freely, forming a great network which collects the vegetation in the water, and gradually convert the swamp into solid land.

# WHY WE SNEEZE?

SNEEZING results from a tickling in the nose, and there are several causes : purposeful tickling with a feather, inhaling dust, a sudden draught of hot or cold air, looking at a dazzling light like the sun, often, having a " cold " and, sometimes, when " cold " germs attack you.

All these things " irritate " the lining of your nose ; the brain orders the body to " sneeze " out the irritating cause. The body obeys by shedding tears, water pouring into your nostrils, a sudden intake of air, and then a violent contraction of all your breathing out muscles—result, you " sneeze " !

# HOW AN ELECTRIC SLOT
# METER WORKS?

**W**HEN the electric light suddenly goes out, you know that it is time to put another shilling in the slot. That is, of course, if you have a slot meter. But how many people realize what a meter actually does in response to the payment?

The illustration shows diagramatically the mechanism of a prepayment electric meter, which consists of four main parts—a motor

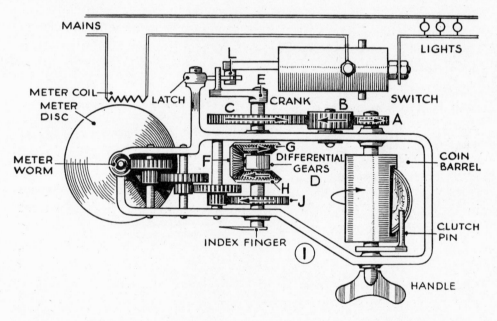

meter, a coin receiving device, a pre-payment mechanism and a switch.

The coin is placed in a slot in a barrel (figures 1 and 2). The handle, when turned, engages, by means of a pin, with the projecting coin, turns the barrel half round and drops the coin in the box below. The barrel is geared by wheels A, B and C with a differential gear D, consisting of a spindle E having at one end a crank and an index finger at the other. Attached to the spindle is an arm carrying a planet wheel F, which gears with two sun wheels G and H attached to sleeves around the spindle E and carrying at their ends gear wheels C and J respectively.

When the coin is inserted, and the handle turned, the gearing A,

B and C drives the upper sun wheel G in the direction of the arrow. The sun wheel H is stationary, so the planet F turns round H and moves the spindle E and its crank and the index finger in a clockwise direction. The index finger thus shows the number of coins inserted.

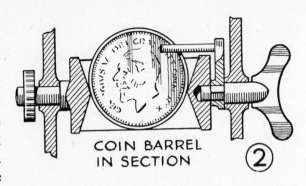

COIN BARREL IN SECTION ②

The meter is represented by the disc with a meter worm (on a vertical shaft) which drives a train of wheels, the last of which, J, is fixed to the sun wheel H. The sun wheel rotates in the opposite direction to the sun wheel G, so that motion of the meter will cancel the motion given G by the handle rotating the coin barrel. Thus, when using current, the crank is turned in a clockwise direction.

The crank controls the position of a latch (figures 1 and 3), which supports a mercury switch mounted on a pivot at K (figure 3) with an extending pin L (figures 1 and 3). The switch is in the closed position and as shown the two terminals of the house wiring are immersed in the mercury and current flows, the switch resting by the pin L on the end of the latch lever. As current is used, the crank is moved in an anti-clockwise direction and eventually engages with the sloping face of the latch, pushes it back and the switch falls and the mercury leaves the terminals and cuts off current.

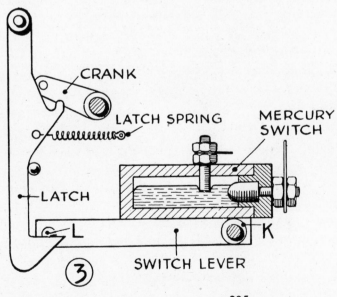

CRANK

LATCH SPRING

MERCURY SWITCH

LATCH

L

③

SWITCH LEVER

K

# WHY LEAVES ARE GREEN?

A RAY of white light when passed through a triangular prism of glass is broken up into rainbow colours.

These seven spectrum colours are displayed in the order : red, orange, yellow, green, blue, indigo, violet. Experiments in growing plants under coloured glass have shown that under the red, orange and yellow colours, leaves are extremely active in manufacturing food materials. Under blue and violet colours little or no starch is formed.

SYCAMORE AND MAPLE LEAVES.

The green pigment in leaves, while absorbing the red and yellow rays, acts as a screen against these blue and violet colours. It, however, rejects the green rays.

Our visual impression of leaves is that they appear green, for we are viewing only the rejected rays.

# WHY WE CATCH COLD?

T HIS is one of those odd sayings which express only half a truth. We really " catch germs " and then, because we feel chilly and get a snuffly nose, say we have " caught cold." This is how and why : everything about us (including the air) is covered with visible or invisible dust to which germs frequently attach themselves. When anyone has a " catching " illness, it means that their bodies are invaded by germs. The " cold " germs settle in the nose and throat. When anybody has " caught a cold," they cough and sneeze, scattering a shower of microbes which, in turn, *you* may breathe into *your* nose and throat. Fortunately we have in our bodies travelling " cells " whose function is to eat up microbes. If you are in perfect health you may thus " resist " the attack, but if you are over-tired or have got wet, your resistance and vitality is lowered—then the germs have a better chance of winning the battle, and you " catch cold." All this teaches us a lesson ; don't go within four feet of people with " colds " ; breathe through the nose ; don't keep your mouth open, because the throat is more liable to infection than the nose—and—don't get wet feet.

# WHAT TREE IS THIS?

CERTAIN birds are called weaver birds because of the wonderful nests which they make. They are found especially in East and West Africa and are remarkable for the fact that the claw of their first toe is very strong and highly curved. When they make their nests, they gather coarse grasses ; the heads of the grass make a bed

A ROOF OF BIRDS' NESTS.

What appears to be a roof built on a tree is the work of South African Sociable Weaver birds, and covers thousands of their tiny nests.

for the young. The grasses they weave into whatever shape they wish.

Some of these birds, rightly called " Sociable," live in colonies under what looks like a big umbrella. This they make together, and afterwards each pair makes its own home under the umbrella ; they are sheltered by the common dome. It is told how these weavers, if they are captured and put into a cage, will go on with their old habits. If cotton or thread is given to them, they will weave it into the bars of the cage. They use their bills as their needle, by means of which they pass the cotton to and fro, while they cling to the sides of the cage with their claws. They are birds of many colours, some of them gorgeous, with long tails ; others are more like one of our finches. But they are all clever weavers.

# WHAT IS A SEA-SERPENT ?

FROM the earliest times sailors have told us of strange creatures which they have seen on their journeys. The chief of these monsters is the sea-serpent, which in the stories of sailors is often like a snake with a red head. It is said to be more than twenty feet long, and it may even be fifty. Along the middle of the back there is a fin which extends all the way to the end. The fins are bright scarlet ; and the fish has a head which might look at a distance like that of a sea-horse. It is probable that the oar-fish is one of the real things which sailors have seen.

THE OAR-FISH IS PROBABLY THE SEA-SERPENT OF THE SAILORS' STORIES.

This ball of lead is floating like a balloon over the two lead rings.   It is supported entirely
by magnetic force generated by electric currents running round the rings.

A CRAFTSMAN MAKING WOODEN WHEELS FOR FARM CARTS.

210

A SOLAR ECLIPSE. [*Royal Astronomical Society.*]

# HOW HOT IS THE SUN?

THE sun is so hot that no known substance within one hundred thousand miles of it can exist in the solid or even in the liquid state. The surface temperature is eleven thousand degrees Fahrenheit, which explains why hard, heavy metals like iron, lead, tin, copper, silver and zinc are boiled into the vaporous state and float as steam and gases in the solar atmosphere, just as oxygen, nitrogen and water vapour float in the earth's atmosphere. The heat from every square foot of surface is sufficient to melt over fifteen hundredweight (three quarters of a ton) of ice per minute. Like any other fire, the sun is far hotter inside than out and its central temperature is estimated to be nearly eighty million degrees Fahrenheit. If, therefore, the comparatively cool outside layers were suddenly removed, the innermost core of the sun would burn the earth and all on it to smoke and ash in little longer than the twinkling of an eye.

# WHY ICE CREAM SODA FROTHS?

EVERYONE must have noticed that an ice cream soda has a way of frothing at the top. That is part of its charm, and the explanation is quite simple. Soda-water is ordinary water with carbon dioxide dissolved in it. That is why it is fizzy. But it contains a lot more gas than you normally see. Add some sugar to a glass of soda-water and much of the gas will come bubbling out. The reason is that carbon dioxide is less soluble in water containing sugar than in ordinary water. Sweetened ice cream, naturally, acts in the same way.

# WHAT CAUSES WIND?

WINDS are air currents and their prime cause is temperature differences, the uneven heating of the earth's surface and atmosphere by the sun.

The extreme north and south polar regions are over sixty degrees Fahrenheit colder than the tropics, the tropic night is often over fifty degrees colder than the tropic day, while for every mile we rise above sea-level the temperature drops about seventeen degrees. Warm air, being lighter, tends to be lifted up and pushed along by colder, heavier air.

Where it is hottest, the air is naturally lightest, and consequently the faster it flies before cooler air-currents which sooner or later rush in till the balance is restored. That is why local heat waves so frequently break up with windy weather and gales. That also is why the tropics and nearby regions are most swept by destructive hurricanes and typhoons ; they are the hottest parts of the globe, and the scene of the most drastic daily temperature changes, themselves capable of setting up furious motions. An old maxim says truly that " night is the winter of the tropics." The chief permanent difference of temperature in the world is, of course, between the torrid (equatorial) zone and the frigid (polar) zones. The atmospheric circulation, therefore, the winds everywhere, ought to be mainly between these two zones, i.e. north-south. This would happen were it not for another important factor—the earth's rotation, which modifies and complicates matters enormously. (See " What are the Trade Winds ? " page 160).

A DEVIL FISH, SEVENTEEN FEET ACROSS AND SEVENTEEN-AND-A-HALF
FEET LONG, WEIGHING JUST UNDER TWO TONS.

# TELL ME, PLEASE?

1.  What do we call " Traveller's joy "?

2.  What is the capital of New Zealand?

3.  What British port is nearest to the equator?

4.  What do we mean by a Roman candle?

5.  What is the year 1666 famous for in England?

6.  What do we mean by a Sally Lunn?

7.  What does K.C. stand for?

8.  What does Q.M.G. stand for?

9.  What is a cardoon?

10. How long is a lawn tennis court?

11. How high is the Great Pyramid?

*Answers to these questions will be found on page 214.*

# ANSWERS TO QUESTIONS on page 213

1. The wild clematis.

2. Wellington.

3. Singapore.

4. A firework that throws out brightly-coloured balls.

5. The Great Fire of London.

6. A kind of teacake that is served hot.

7. King's Counsel.

8. Quartermaster-General.

9. A vegetable, something like an artichoke.

10. Seventy-eight feet.

11. Four hundred and eighty feet.

[*Aerofilms, Ltd.*

MONTMORENCY FALLS, SEVEN MILES FROM QUEBEC CITY AND TWO
HUNDRED AND EIGHTY FEET HIGH.

*By courtesy of* [*Cadbury Bros.*

OPENING COCOA PODS.

# WHAT IS COCOA?

COCOA is made from the seeds of several kinds of palm trees which grow in tropical America and in other warm climates. Linnaeus, the celebrated Swedish botanist, gave the name of " Theobroma " to this kind of palm, which means " the food of the gods," and you will agree, I expect, that a cup of steaming cocoa with plenty of sugar and milk is a very delicious supper drink. When the almond-shaped seeds are taken from the pods in which they grow, they are very bitter, but they lose this unpleasant flavour whilst they are stored in heaps on the ground or in earthen vessels. The matured seeds are cleaned and sorted and then roasted in revolving drums ; next they are gently crushed to remove the thin outer shell, and the remaining beans are called cocoa nibs. These are ground to a very fine powder under heavy rollers, but before this is packed in tins for you to buy, a great deal of fatty matter, known as cocoa butter and used in medicine, is removed. Some kinds of cocoa have all the " butter " removed, and then if you have a sweet tooth, you will want to put several extra lumps of sugar in your cup of cocoa. It is interesting to know that the broken and roasted shells are not wasted, but are ground and made into a sort of cheap "coffee" sold in Italy and Spain and which is called " miserabile."

THE ARCTIC FOX IN WINTER.    [*Carthew & Kinnaird, Ltd.*

# WHY SOME ANIMALS AND BIRDS WEAR WHITE IN WINTER?

THERE are certain animals and birds which gradually become white as winter approaches.

In the northern parts of Scotland the familiar brown stoat of southern England becomes the pure white ermine. Likewise, the mountain hare in Scotland is white, while in Ireland it retains its bluish-grey colour. Neither of these animals, however, turns entirely white, for the stoat retains the black tip of its tail, and the hare the black tip on its ears.

The Arctic fox, which used to occur in Britain, but is now not found nearer than Iceland, behaves in the same manner, as also does the mountain lemming of Scandinavia.

Turning to birds, there is the white ptarmigan, together with the willow grouse, both of the mountains of Scotland, which change their summer chestnut-browns to grey in autumn, and snowy white in winter.

This adaptation to whiteness suggests that it serves to render these creatures inconspicuous amidst their snowy surroundings, and probably, to some extent, it does function in that way, but there may be other reasons than that of invisibility.

Since these animals are by no means always amidst snowy

216

# WHY ANIMALS WEAR WHITE IN WINTER ?

surroundings, there are times when they become extremely conspicuous. When, in the absence of snow, the white hare crosses a ploughed field, or the ermine climbs a rock, these animals become more strikingly visible than ever they would be in their summer coats.

Probably the real reason why these animals and birds become white is a physiological one. There is much evidence to show that white hairs and white feathers are developed to retain warmth.

Whiteness means economy in loss of animal heat, and, as winter approaches, the pigment granules of hairs and feathers tend to be absorbed into the body.

The space which should have been occupied by the pigment grains, then becomes filled with tiny gas bubbles, which, collectively, reflect so many light rays, that the hairs and feathers appear white —just as snow does from the reflections of its numerous tiny crystals.

Some of the creatures that live more or less in the Arctic Circle, like the polar bear, white whale, snowy owl, and Greenland falcon, remain white throughout the year.

While, therefore, winter whiteness may suggest camouflage as its obvious explanation, it may have a much greater significance.

[Dorien Leigh, Ltd.

WEARING HIS WINTER COAT.

[*Mirrorpic.*

THE OBJECT OF THIS SCHOOL ORCHESTRA IS TO PRODUCE
HARMONIOUS SOUNDS.

# WHAT IS NOISE?

WE all know a noise when we hear it ; but what is it ? Well, first of all it is sound, but not all sounds are noise. A noise is really a complicated sound in which various wavelengths or sounds of different pitch have become mixed up. If you strike a glass, you hear a " pure " musical note, but if you drop half-a-dozen on the floor, you will get a hundred different sounds that produce a noise.

Really, we can almost define noise by saying that it is sound out of place. A drum gives a musical note in a concert hall when it is played at the right moment, but if it crashed in at the wrong moment or is played by your next-door neighbour at midnight, you would say " What a noise ! " Some sounds which in themselves are not unpleasant produce a " noise " when they mix or fail to " combine."

One thing we do know is that noise is bad for us. We may think we are becoming accustomed to it, but all the time it is doing harm. When a test was carried out, it was found that people working in a noisy room were, on an average, twenty-five per cent less efficient than people working in a silent room.

# WHAT IS NOISE ?

We now have a means of measuring the intensity of noise, the standard of measurement being called a decibel. Ten decibels is a quiet whisper ; twenty decibels, the average of a very quiet street ; fifty decibels, cars passing with the windows shut or ordinary conversation in a room ; and so we go up to ninety decibels for a pneumatic drill and one hundred and ten decibels for a noisy aeroplane.

[B.O.A.C.

**AN ABYSSINIAN HARPIST PLAYING AT THE FEAST OF EPIPHANY.**

# DO "CANDLES" GROW ON TREES?

IN some parts of South Africa may be found the extraordinary species of tree shown in our illustration, *Sarcocaulon rigidum*, commonly known as " The Bushman's Candle." This weird-looking, spiky plant owes its peculiar name to the fact that it is literally covered with long candle-like spikes and that the stems of the young plant can be lit and will then burn like a candle.

In some of the forests of the Isthmus of Panama, Central America, is found another weird-looking Candle Tree (*Parmentiera cereifera*).

From its branches are suspended what appear to be hundreds of huge candles. These are three to four feet in length, of a yellow wax colour, and do actually yield fat to the extent of about half their weight.

These so-called candles are really the fruits of the tree, and they bear lentil-like seeds. They have an apple-like smell, and provide food for cattle. Unless this food is changed for a few days before the killing of the cattle, the apple odour is communicated to the flesh of the animals.

[*Carthew & Kinnaird, Ltd.*

THE BUSHMAN'S CANDLE (*SARCOCAULON RIGIDUM*).

ROWING WITH HIS FEET.

The natives of the South Shan States, Burma, and other Eastern people, propel their craft, often at extraordinary speed in this manner.

# TELL ME, PLEASE?

1. What is the name of the highest mountain in the British Isles.
2. Where is the Dead Sea?
3. What country do we call the " Land of the Midnight Sun "?
4. What is the length, in feet, of a fathom?
5. What is a Begum?
6. What is correctly called the right bank of a river?
7. What is an agouti?
8. What and where is Arthur's Seat?
9. What do we mean by Savanna?
10. What is a samovar?
11. What is the port side of a ship?
12. Where was King Arthur born?
13. What is the derivation of the word " tantalize "?
14. Who invented printing?

*Answers to these questions will be found on page 222.*

# ANSWERS TO QUESTIONS on page 221

1. Ben Nevis.
2. In Palestine.
3. Norway.
4. Six.
5. An Indian lady of high rank.
6. The right bank when standing facing the river mouth.
7. An animal of the guinea-pig kind from South America.
8. The site of a long-extinct volcano, overlooking Edinburgh.
9. A greasy plain.
10. A Russian hot-water urn.
11. The left side.
12. Tintagel Castle, Cornwall.
13. From the mythical figure Tantalus, who was sentenced to stand in water that he was never allowed to drink.
14. Gutenberg of Germany.

[Tea Bureau.

**A SINGHALESE POTTER AT WORK.**

THE GREAT STAR CLUSTER IN HERCULES.

# HOW MANY STARS ARE THERE?

NEVER more than five thousand stars are visible at once to the naked eye. A telescope with a lens five inches across will reveal about nine millions, while with the largest spyglass at present in the world, the hundred-inch mirror at Mount Wilson Observatory, over one thousand two hundred millions have been photographed. Long-exposure photographs prove that a little patch of faint, milky light in the constellation Hercules is really a magnificent cluster of over one hundred thousand suns, each brighter than our sun. The great sun, which warms and lights the whole earth, is only one of a galaxy or huge family of stars (for the sun is just the nearest star to the earth), estimated to number between ten thousand million and one hundred thousand million. And there are millions of other galaxies or star families. In other words, if all the stars in the universe were grains of sand, there would be enough of them to cover the whole of Britain over fifty yards deep.

# WHAT IS A SEA-MOUSE?

IT is not really a mouse at all; to find an account of it in books of natural history, we must not look to the section dealing with mice, but to the worm-like animals, and among them to the group with many bristles. One sea-mouse lives near the British shores; it is broad-bodied and somewhat like a slug, the enemy against which the gardener is always fighting. It is about three or four inches long. If we find it and take the trouble to remove from its

[*John J. Ward.*

A SEA-MOUSE.

Its silky hairs gleam with all the colours of the rainbow. It is really a sea-worm and has a ringed body.
The picture shows the underside.

skin the mud and sand with which it is covered, we shall see it bright with varied colours—a little like those of the rainbow. The back has a double row of scales overlapping one another; but those we find on our British shores are wrapped in a covering of hairs, but there are sea-mice in the Mediterranean without such hairs. It might be supposed that such a creature, with its protection of spines, would be safe from its greedy enemies. But it is not; and fish of various kinds, such as the cod and the haddock, look upon the sea-mouse as good food, and do not mind the spines or the bristles shaped like arrows.